Fenianism in Mid-Victorian Brit

A Socialist History of Britain

Series edited by the Northern Marxist Historians Group

Kieran Allen, *Fianna Fail and Irish Labour: from Populism to Corporatism*

John Saville, *The Consolidation of the Capitalist State, 1800–1850*

Fenianism in
Mid-Victorian Britain

John Newsinger

Pluto Press

LONDON · BOULDER, COLORADO

First published 1994 by Pluto Press
345 Archway Road, London N6 5AA
and 5500 Central Avenue
Boulder, Colorado 80301, USA

British Library Cataloguing in Publication Data
A catalogue record for this book is available from the British
Library

Library of Congress Cataloging in Publication Data
Newsinger, John, 1948–
    Fenians in mid-victorian Britain / John Newsinger.
        p.   cm. — (Socialist history of Britain)
    Includes index
    ISBN 0–7453–0900–3
    1. Fenians. 2. Ireland—History—1837–1901. I. Title.
    II. Series.
    DA954.N48 1995
    940.7081—dc20   94–32946
                                                                              CIP

ISBN   0 7453 0900 3 Hardback

A Socialist History of Britain
ISSN 1353 – 5021

98   97   96   95   94
  5   4   3   2   1

Designed and produced for Pluto Press by
Chase Production Services, Chipping Norton, OX7 5QR
Typeset from author's disk by Stanford DTP Services
Printed in the EC

Contents

For Lorna

Acknowledgements

The analysis and argument presented in this study have been developed over the last two decades in a number of journals: *Race and Class, European Studies Review, Eire–Ireland, Literature and History* and *Saothar*, to which I am grateful. More particularly I am grateful to Colin Barker, David Howell and Emmet O'Connor for their criticism and advice. They do not, of course, bear any responsibility for any mistakes or errors in the account presented here. An especial mention must be made for Margaret Tremeer, my typist, who good-humouredly fitted me in among a mountain of other work.

Introduction

The Fenian movement was one of the most important of the revolutionary movements that challenged the British Empire in the nineteenth century. It successfully dominated Irish popular politics in the 1860s, defying the anathemas of the Catholic Church and the condemnations of respectable middle-class nationalists to organise rebellion against British rule. Thousands of young Irishmen, both in Ireland itself and on the British mainland, were recruited into its ranks. It successfully infiltrated the British army, and although the best opportunity for a rising was missed in 1865 nevertheless in 1867 it made an unsuccessful attempt to launch a revolutionary war. This effort was to provide the movement with its own collection of heroes and martyrs, men who endured prison or who died on the scaffold for the cause of national freedom. The Fenians made a little-known attempt to ally themselves with British Radicals who were at this time conducting an aggressive campaign for the vote, through the Reform League agitation. They received support from their sister revolutionary organisation in the United States of America, which provided them with funds, munitions and men for the struggle in Ireland and even attempted to invade Canada. Despite its defeat at the hands of the British, Fenianism was without doubt the most important force in Irish politics in the 1860s; moreover, it compelled the British political establishment to initiate reforms that began the final destruction of the Protestant ascendancy. Certainly at the time both Karl Marx and Friedrich Engels recognised the importance of the movement – not just for Ireland but for Britain as well.

How to write the history of this movement? The traditional nationalist interpretation is to regard it as an episode in the Irish people's unbroken tradition of struggle against British rule that goes back 800 years. This tradition is in fact an ideological construct, a manufactured history that was invented to give legitimacy to the modern nationalist cause. It celebrates a mythical past rather than helping to understand the actual development of Irish society. Rather than an unbroken tradition, what we have in reality is a series of distinct movements of opposition to English, later British, rule that were the product of specific conditions and circumstances. The O'Neill rebellion of the 1590s, the great rebellion of the 1640s, the

United Irish rebellion of the 1790s and the Fenian movement of the 1860s have very little in common with each other and are certainly not part of a continuous movement of resistance to British rule. The O'Neill rebellion might have inspired the Fenians, but their democratic movement was radically different from the aristocratic resistance of the lords of Gaelic Ulster. This is even true of the United Irish revolt of 1798, which was separated from the Fenians by a dramatic transformation in Irish society. Whereas the United Irish movement had been initiated by Protestant dissenters and had its organisational centre in the north, by the 1860s the north and most Protestant dissenters had embraced the Union. At the same time, Catholic Ireland had been transformed by the Great Famine that had dramatically reduced the number of Irish poor by starvation and emigration and had increased the social weight of the better-off farmers of the rural middle class. The Fenians might well have looked to Wolfe Tone, but their movement was very different from the movement that he had addressed and the Ireland they hoped to liberate was very different from the Ireland he intended to set free.

Much the same point can be made with regard to the republican movement at the time of the Easter Rising of 1916 or of the Provisional IRA today. Both look to the Fenians as predecessors and take inspiration from that movement's history; but rather than seeing them as descended in an unbroken line from the Fenians of the 1860s, it is more useful to regard them as distinct movements that have arisen in specific circumstances. They are connected in the sense that they draw on a common political tradition and ideology, but the differences are if anything more important. The working-class Irish Republican Brotherhood of the 1860s, with its mass membership, was very different from the small middle-class Irish Republican Brotherhood of 1916 that operated through front organisations. Both of these were in turn very different from the working-class IRA of today, which operates in an advanced industrial society characterised by sectarian divisions of a ferocity not evident in the 1860s or in 1916. Any history of the republican tradition has to be concerned with the differences between these movements, as well as with the elements of continuity.

While the nationalist tradition can be seen to be inadequate as an account of Fenianism, what has come to replace it in recent years, the so-called revisionist interpretation, is hardly an improvement. Within the context of Irish history, revisionism has involved historians subjecting the history of Irish nationalism to a critical and often sceptical scrutiny, concerned to strip away the 'myths' that have grown up around the national struggle. As far as Fenianism is concerned, revisionism, most closely associated with the work of R.V. Comerford since the early 1980s, has contributed a great deal to our empirical knowledge of the movement, but as far as explanation goes it is compromised by a conservative hostility towards Radicalism and revolution. This has resulted in the denigration of the Fenian movement, in an attempt to minimalise its importance and dilute its revolutionary character. Such an exercise is very much part of the general shift to the right in the western world, and more specifically of the rejection of physical-force republicanism that has emerged in response to the war in Northern Ireland. It does not, as we shall see, do justice to the Fenians.

What this study attempts is to situate the Fenian movement of the 1860s in the context of Irish politics and society, recognising it as a revolutionary democratic movement of national liberation, but also to restore it to its place in nineteenth-century British history and in the history of the British Empire.

CHAPTER 1

1848 in Ireland

The Great Famine

Writing an 'Introductory' to his celebrated *Jail Journal* in 1854, John Mitchel looked back from his American exile at the years of the Great Famine in Ireland:

> At the end of six years, I can set down these things calmly; but to see them might have driven a wise man mad ... how families, when all was eaten and no hope left, took their last look at the Sun, built up their cottage doors that none might see them die nor hear their groans, and were found weeks afterwards skeletons on their own hearth; how the 'law' was vindicated all this while; how the Arms Bills were diligently put in force, and many examples were made; how the starving were transported for stealing vegetables ...[1]

This, he hoped, would 'explain the contumacy and inveterately rebellious spirit evident enough in the pages' of his *Journal*. Indeed, this not only explains the ferocity of his book; it is also crucial to an understanding of the revival of Irish republicanism in the late 1840s, a revival to which Mitchel himself made a considerable contribution.

The Great Famine was caused by the combination of potato blight (the fungus *Phytophthora infectans*), the Irish social structure and British rule. The first caused the failure of the potato crop, but it was the second and third that were responsible for this failure resulting in the literal decimation of the Irish population.

The blight first appeared in 1845, when it destroyed between 30 and 40 per cent of Ireland's potato crop, the staple of the poor, creating severe shortages and considerable hardship. The following year almost the entire crop was destroyed and hardship turned to grim famine. In 1847 the effects of the blight were less severe, but the peasantry had already consumed what seed potatoes they had, so that harvest yields were only 10 per cent of what they had been in 1844. The following year, 1848, the blight returned once again to devastate the crop. This catastrophe was to continue into the early 1850s, with potato yields still remaining at only half the pre-Famine level.

What were the effects of this natural calamity? Around one million people, citizens of the United Kingdom, died of starvation, disease or exposure in western Europe's worst modern peacetime disaster. Overwhelmingly, it was the poor who died – the small farmers, cottiers and landless labourers – and disproportionately it was the women and children from these social groups who were affected. South Ulster, west Munster and Connaught were the areas worst affected, but every district where subsistence farming predominated suffered terribly. Even the Wicklow mountains, in sight of Dublin, were devastated by hunger and disease. While thousands starved and died, as many fled the country as refugees, emigrating for their very lives to Britain and to America. Over a million people emigrated during the Great Famine, many carrying with them a bitter hatred of British rule.

A major cause of the scale of the disaster was the sheer number of the poor in Ireland. The population increased from around five million in 1800 to over eight million in 1840, with an increasing proportion living in poverty. This was partly due to the potato. It was this crop's ability to support a family on a small acreage that made possible the extent of subdivision and subletting in Ireland. By the 1840s some four million people were mainly dependent on the potato for sustenance, two million of them completely so. That the potato had this impact in Ireland, however, was not due to some Malthusian inevitability but to the system of landholding. The land was overwhelmingly owned by Protestant landlords, most of whom had either no interest in or no capital for agricultural improvements. They were concerned with extracting rents, and increasing the number of tenants was often the quickest way to achieve this. These men have figured, with considerable justification, as the major villains of the piece in traditional nationalist accounts.

In fact, there was another exploiting stratum between these men and the poor, a small rural middle class of substantial (by Irish standards) Catholic tenant-farmers who rented farms of 30 acres or more, engaged in commercial farming and employed some labour. These comparatively well-to-do farmers were the backbone of O'Connell's Catholic Emancipation and Repeal movements and of the reviving Catholic Church. According to the 1841 census, seven per cent of farms covered more than 30 acres. Below this group were the growing numbers of the rural poor, the small farmers, cottiers and labourers whose holdings were either altogether incapable of or only barely able to support their families. Once again according to the 1841 census, an astonishing 45 per cent of farms were less than five acres in size. There was, of course, considerable regional variation; so that in Connaught, for example, the proportion of farms under five acres was as high as 64 per cent.

Many of the better-off farmers aped the landlords by subletting their poorest land at exorbitant rents. This provided both income and ready access to cheap labour. The scale of impoverishment is, however, best demonstrated by the fact that in the 1840s some 40 per cent of the houses in Ireland were one-room mud cabins. Many more were little better.

What was the official response to the Great Famine? The first partial failure of the potato crop in 1845 was met by limited relief measures which were nevertheless on a sufficient scale to ensure that few actually starved to death. The complete failure of the crop the following year coincided with the replacement of Sir Robert Peel's interventionist Tory administration by a Whig administration headed by Lord John Russell. This new government was doctrinally committed to laissez-faire, free trade and market forces, even to the extent of refusing to prohibit the export of food from Ireland, a measure that without any doubt would have saved tens of thousands of lives. It ended Peel's food relief measures and subsidies to Irish public works, throwing the whole cost of public works on to the backs of Irish ratepayers who were, of course, crippled by the Famine, and leaving the provision of food to the free market. The results were disastrous and the government was reluctantly and grudgingly forced to adopt emergency measures. The public works programme was overwhelmed by the scale of the catastrophe: the numbers employed increased from 250,000 in the autumn of 1846 to three-quarters of a million in the spring of 1847. When this expedient collapsed it was replaced by a resort to soup kitchens which by August 1847 were feeding three million people a day. This was only intended as a stop-gap measure while the government introduced a workhouse system across Ireland. All these measures were implemented in a mean-spirited, parsimonious fashion, with the lead being given by the Chancellor of the Exchequer, Sir Charles Wood, and the Under-Secretary at the Treasury, Sir Charles Trevelyan. In effect, a million people died because government relief measures were too little and too late. Even in the closing stages of the Famine, relief measures were only successful in keeping down the death toll because so many of the poor were already dead or had fled the country.

The Irish poor were sacrificed on the altar of financial orthodoxy. It has been argued, of course, that those responsible, the Whig ministers and their officials, did in fact do all that they believed it was possible to do. The ideological universe these men inhabited, so the argument goes, simply did not provide solutions to the scale of the problem they found themselves facing. This is not a convincing excuse. It frees their ideas from the social and political context in which they were formed. Their ideological system had not appeared out of nowhere; rather it had been invented, created, by them to represent their interests. The problem was not that their ideology could not provide solutions, but rather that the Famine did not affect their interests sufficiently for them to change their ideas. A crucial factor here is undoubtedly Ireland's colonial status. If a similar calamity had affected part of mainland Britain, there can be no doubt that the consequent threat to the social and political order would have ensured action to prevent mass starvation whatever the prevailing orthodoxy. Mass starvation in Ireland was just not an important enough issue for British politicians. Moreover, Ireland was already perceived as a hotbed of disaffection, and if anything the Famine, as we shall see, actually helped preserve British rule rather than posing a threat to it.

What of the expense? Could the government have afforded to keep alive a million Irish men, women and children? Altogether the British government spent some £7 million on famine relief. This contrasts uncomfortably with the £20 million given to slave-owners in the West Indies to compensate them for emancipation some years earlier, or with the £70 million later spent on the Crimean War.

Eviction

One last aspect of the Great Famine requires mention here: mass starvation was accompanied by mass evictions. The government not only failed to feed the starving but also stood by, indeed assisted with its police and troops, while they were thrown off the land and their homes were destroyed. For many this was tantamount to a sentence of death. Thousands abandoned their land after the 'Gregory clause' of March 1847, named after the Irish landlord who proposed it, denied relief to anyone holding more than a quarter acre of land. Others were forcibly evicted. The number of evictions rose dramatically in 1847 and continued to rise every year until 1850, still remaining high in 1851 and 1852. It is impossible to calculate exact figures of the number of people evicted, not least because police figures understate the number of evictions carried out, but a total of half a million people is probably not excessive. Police figures for 1849 to 1854 alone give an official total of over 248,000 people evicted. The sheer scale of this clearance at a time of mass starvation is staggering. In County Clare a tenth of the population were evicted and in Galway and Kerry the proportion was not much lower.

While the countryside was starving and the land was being cleared, the Irish upper class continued a life of splendid luxury. As John Mitchel subsequently observed, Dublin was throughout the Famine 'extremely gay and beautiful'. He added:

you may imagine that Dublin city would show some effect or symptom of such a national calamity. Singular to relate that city had never before been so gay and luxurious; splendid equipages had never before so crowded the streets; and the theatres and concert rooms had never been filled with such brilliant throngs ... Any stranger arriving in those days, guided by judicious friends only through fashionable streets and squares, introduced only to proper circles, would have said that Dublin must be the prosperous capital of some wealthy and happy country.[2]

The Viceroy, Lord Clarendon, at the same time as presiding over the starvation and coercion of rural Ireland, also presided over Dublin's social life. In February 1848 there were three large balls at Dublin Castle, glittering affairs attended by 1,300, 400 and 45 guests respectively, and five large dinner parties. The following month saw two balls for 900 and 550 guests and four large dinner parties. Only someone completely disaffected could possibly see anything untoward in all this.

What of the social consequences of this catastrophe? We shall look at this in more detail later, but it is worth making the point here that while the Great Famine killed or drove overseas a substantial proportion of the Irish poor (the number of landless labourers fell by 28 per cent and the number of small farmers with holdings of five acres or less by 40–50 per cent between 1841 and 1851), the Catholic rural middle class actually increased in numbers and in social weight. Instead of farms of 30 acres or more comprising only seven per cent of total landholdings, by 1851 these accounted for 26 per cent. These well-to-do farmers emerged from the Famine as the dominant social group among the Catholic population in Ireland.

Young Ireland

Throughout the 1840s the maintenance of law and order in Ireland was a source of constant concern to British governments. Disorder and rebellion seemed ever-present possibilities that could only be contained by the threat of armed force and repression. In the early part of the decade, Daniel O'Connell's massive Repeal movement had been seen as posing a serious challenge to British rule in Ireland, his militant rhetoric concealing, at least from his followers, an absolute commitment to constitutional methods. Whatever O'Connell's own commitment, there was always a danger that the mass movement he led might escape his control. The Peel government resolved to crush it, banning the planned Clontarf rally in October 1843 and then, after O'Connell had backed down, prosecuting him for treason before a packed jury.

O'Connell's failure to offer any resistance to the British caused considerable disillusion within the ranks of the Repeal movement.

At the centre of this discontent were the nationalist intellectuals grouped around *The Nation* newspaper. These men, Charles Gavan Duffy, Thomas Davis, John Mitchel and others, were to become known collectively as 'Young Ireland'. They were romantic cultural and literary nationalists who had willingly followed O'Connell, but were now finding his eagerness to make deals with British Whig politicians and his robust pacifism insupportable. Their cause was greatly strengthened by the adherence of William Smith O'Brien MP, O'Connell's only serious rival in the Repeal Association.

Disappointment with O'Connell's retreat at Clontarf was eventually to culminate in a split in the Repeal Association in July 1846 and the establishment of the rival Irish Confederation in January 1847. In many ways the new organisation was little more than the old Repeal Association minus O'Connell and his willingness to ally with the Whigs. It was not a revolutionary organisation and while it steadfastly refused to rule out the use of force in response to British tyranny, this did not involve any commitment actually to use force to secure Irish independence. From the very beginning, the Irish Confederation was itself divided over how to respond to the crisis of the Great Famine.

'Young Ireland' had in many respects been conservative in its social outlook: Duffy, Davis and co. had made the conversion of the Protestant landlords to the nationalist cause the cornerstone of their political strategy. The movement they hoped to build would be more like the constitutional volunteer movement of 1782 than the revolutionary United Irishmen of 1798; and the independent Ireland they hoped to create would be a harmonious rural community where landlords fulfilled their social obligations to a grateful tenantry that acknowledged their natural claim to leadership. The Famine with its mass starvation and wholesale evictions shattered this idyllic vision for a number of Young Irelanders, most notably John Mitchel, who moved dramatically to the left.

Mitchel was much influenced in his response to the Famine by the writings of another Young Irelander, James Fintan Lalor, the son of one of the leading figures in the Tithe Wars of the 1830s, who had forcefully argued that Repeal was not the cause to arouse the peasantry to revolt and that only the struggle for the land was close enough to their hearts. Mitchel embraced this doctrine of social revolution with considerable reluctance: instead of looking to the landlords for leadership they were now to be forcibly dispossessed in the fight for national independence. Much later, when he recalled these times, he argued that such a social revolution could 'only be justified by desperate necessity' and that the Great Famine had constituted such a necessity. He wrote that 'when the system was found to work so fatally – when hundreds of thousands of people were lying down and perishing ... society itself stood dissolved'.[3]

Such a form of society was 'not only a failure, but an intolerable oppression, and cried aloud to be cut up by the roots and swept away'. Only bloody revolution could reconstitute it on a new foundation. Mitchel's new-found radicalism also led him to reconsider his attitude towards British Chartism: instead of a democratic contagion that Ireland should avoid, the Chartists were now seen as allies in the struggle to bring the British Empire crashing down.

The United Irishman

Mitchel's extreme viewpoint remained that of a militant minority within the Irish Confederation and he soon defected from the organisation to launch his own newspaper, the *United Irishman*. This remarkable publication appealed directly to the 'men of no property' and openly advocated armed resistance to the British. The first issue appeared on 12 February 1848. It had as its editorial an open letter to the Viceroy, Lord Clarendon, who was addressed as the 'Englishman; calling himself Her Majesty's Lord Lieutenant General and General Governor of Ireland'. Mitchel promised him that 'the deep and irreconcilable disaffection of this people to all British laws, lawgivers and law administrators shall find a voice' and that it was to the education of 'that holy hatred, to make it know itself, and avow itself, and, at last, fill itself full, I hereby devote the columns of the *United Irishman*'. This was a deliberate and self-conscious attempt to revive the revolutionary spirit of the United Irish movement of the 1790s, to reconstitute Irish republicanism after its bloody suppression in 1798 and the execution of Robert Emmet in 1803.

The newspaper was an immediate success, achieving a circulation of some 10,000 copies and causing the authorities considerable alarm. Interestingly enough, Lord Clarendon's concern was shared by the Confederation's moderate leadership: Charles Gavan Duffy wrote to William Smith O'Brien describing his vision of how 'you and I will meet on a Jacobin scaffold, ordered for execution as enemies of some new Marat or Robespierre, Mr James Lalor or Mr Somebody else!'[4]

Mitchel and his small band of followers determined on a policy of confrontation come what may. As he was later to recall, they were all possessed by a kind of 'sacred wrath ... They could endure the horrible scene no longer, and resolved to cross the path of the British car of conquest, though it should crush them to atoms.'[5] They hoped by their intransigent extremism to force the government into taking repressive measures against them and thereby provoke an armed uprising of the Confederate clubs and a general rebellion.

The moderation of the Confederate leadership would be over-whelmed by the force of circumstances. A crucial factor in their thinking was an alliance with the British Chartists. Hitherto, O'Connell and the Repeal movement had been bitterly hostile to Chartism, had rejected Chartist offers of friendship and opposed Chartists' attempts to extend their influence among the Irish in Britain or to Ireland itself. Relations between O'Connell and the Chartist leader, Feargus O'Connor, himself an Irishman, were characterised by bitter enmity. Despite this, Chartism had made some headway among the Dublin artisans, and Irish Chartists were involved in the Confederate clubs established in the capital. Mitchel and his followers embraced the Chartist cause as their own and set about establishing a secret revolutionary alliance with its more militant wing in Britain.

When the news arrived in Ireland of the revolutionary overthrow of the regime of Louis Philippe in Paris in February 1848, presaging a great revolutionary upsurge throughout Europe, Mitchel enthu-siastically welcomed it and hoped that the contagion would spread to Ireland. In his 'Letter to the Small Farmers of Ireland' that was published in the *United Irishman* on 4 March, he proclaimed:

> The earth is awakening from sleep: a flash of electric fire is passing through the dumb millions. Democracy is girding himself once more like a strong man to run a race; and slumbering nations are arising in their might, and 'shaking their invincible locks'. Oh! my countrymen, look up, look up! Arise from the death-dust where you have long been lying, and let this light visit your eyes also, and touch your souls. Let your ears drink in the blessed words, 'Liberty! Fraternity! Equality!' which are soon to ring from pole to pole. Clear steel will, ere long, dawn upon you in your desolate darkness; and the rolling thunder of the people's cannon will drive before it many a heavy cloud that has long hidden from you the face of heaven. Pray for that day; and preserve life and health that you may worthily greet it. Above all, let the man amongst you who has no gun, sell his garment and buy one.

With the success of revolution in France, even the moderate leadership of the Confederation was tempted. Duffy came to the conclusion that a revolutionary outbreak in Ireland was probably inevitable and that if it was not led by men like himself, then it would be led by the likes of Mitchel and Lalor and would develop into a social war, into a war against the landlords.

How effective was Mitchel's thrilling call to arms? Certainly in Dublin, where the Confederate clubs were dominated by the artisan trades, serious preparations for rebellion were put underway. Arms were collected and large determined bands of men, sometimes 500 strong, paraded through the streets to attend meetings and cheer violent speeches preaching revolution, the Chartist alliance and solidarity with the revolutionary struggle in Europe. On 21 March some 20,000 people attended a meeting at the North Wall, organised by the Dublin trades and addressed by Smith O'Brien, Duffy, Mitchel and others. There was an expectation that the meeting would be banned, and that when the organisers refused to back down troops would be used to disperse it. The resulting clashes might have well precipitated a revolutionary outbreak in Dublin similar to that in Paris the previous month. In fact, Clarendon refused the bait; instead of suppressing the meeting, he proceeded to prosecute Duffy, Thomas Francis Meagher and Mitchel for sedition. The first two prosecutions miscarried through the failure to pack the juries effectively, and both Duffy and Meagher were acquitted. When Mitchel came to trial nothing was left to chance.

Mitchel was arrested on 13 May 1848. He confidently expected that his trial would now prove the occasion for insurrection. His intransigence and uncompromising extremism had at last succeeded in provoking the government into a repressive response and now its blatant jury-rigging would in turn provoke rebellion, or so he hoped. On 16 May he wrote in his cell that 'my work is nearly done'. As far as he was concerned the *United Irishman* had successfully scattered the doctrine of 'moral force ... to the wild winds of heaven'. Beyond his cell, he could hear 'just dying away, the measured tramp of ten thousand marching men – my gallant confederates, unarmed and silent, but with hearts like bended bow, waiting till the time comes'. 'The game', he wrote, 'is afoot at last', and sooner or later he expected to hear 'the crash of the downfall of the thrice-accursed British Empire'.[6]

What Mitchel and his supporters intended was a rescue attempt at the climax of his trial, an attempt that if successful would, they believed, raise Dublin in arms and give the city its own 'days of the barricades'. There can be little doubt that Mitchel's following among Dublin's artisans was large and determined enough for a serious attempt to have been mounted. Instead they were persuaded by Smith O'Brien, Duffy and others that the time was not ripe, that they should wait until the autumn and the harvest was in. The argument went on long into the night of 26 May and the early morning of the 27th before counsels of patience prevailed and the planned rescue was abandoned. Later on the 27 May, Mitchel was sentenced to 14 years' transportation. After hearing his sentence, he asked the friends and associates who packed the court gallery which of them could he pledge to continue the struggle. The scene was graphically described by Alexander Sullivan, a moderate nationalist and no friend of Mitchel's extremism:

As he uttered these closing words he pointed first to John Martin, then to Devin Reilly, next to Thomas Francis Meagher, and so on to the throng of associates whom he saw crowding the galleries. A thundering cry rang through the building. 'Promise for me, Mitchel! Promise for me!' and a rush was made to embrace him ere they should see him no more. The officers in wild dismay thought it meant a rescue. Arms were drawn; bugles in the street outside sounded the alarm; troops hurried up. A number of police flung themselves on Mitchel, tore him from the embrace of his excited friends, and hurried him through the wicket that leads from the dock to the cells beneath.

There seems some justice to Sullivan's judgement that at this moment 'the Irish insurrectionary movement of 1848 was put down'. The decisive opportunity had been missed and what was to follow was an anti-climax.[7]

Within a few hours, Mitchel was taken in chains and under military escort to the North Wall, where he was embarked on a government steamer that carried him off on the first stage of his journey to Van Dieman's Land, now Tasmania. He was not to return to Ireland for more than 25 years.

The sympathy that by now existed between the Irish Confederates and the British Chartists was dramatically demonstrated by a series of marches and protest meetings in London, which culminated in over 50,000 people, British and Irish, protesting against Mitchel's sentence on 29 May. The following day the police banned any further meetings, but their edict was defied. A succession of demonstrations and clashes between Chartists and the police continued until a 'police riot' took place at Bishop Bonner's Field on 4 June. After this outbreak, the government moved to prosecute the Chartist leaders. Among them was Ernest Jones, who had publicly pledged that 'John Mitchel shall be brought back to his native country, and Sir G Grey and Lord John Russell shall be sent out to exchange places with him.'[8] This was to help earn him two years' imprisonment. All through these events and for some time afterwards, the prospect of an Irish outbreak spilling over on to the British mainland was a continuing worry for the government. The defeat of Chartism in the course of 1848 was to be a serious blow to the Confederates who had placed considerable hopes in the Chartist alliance.

The Revolt

After Mitchel's deportation the Confederates established a small committee to prepare for insurrection. Hope of raising Dublin was abandoned in view of the number of troops filling the city

(11,000 soldiers and 1,100 police), and instead it was planned to launch the rebellion in the country. The conspirators were overtaken by events. On 25 July 1848 Habeas Corpus was suspended in Ireland, taking the Confederate leaders completely by surprise. That Clarendon might strike first seems not to have occurred to them. Faced with imminent arrest, they took to the field; in Meagher's words, plunging 'headlong and bewildered, into a system of resistance for which the country was very far from being sufficiently prepared'.[9] They set out to raise the standard of revolt in Kilkenny town, hoping to take control of south-east Tipperary and west Kilkenny and then spread the rebellion throughout the counties of Waterford, Kilkenny and Tipperary. The plan itself was quite promising. The area chosen was ideal for guerrilla warfare and had a strong tradition of secret society activity and agrarian resistance. Its execution was to be disastrous.

When the Confederate leaders arrived in Kilkenny town on 23 July, they found the organisation much weaker than they had been led to believe: it consisted of some 500 men, of whom only 100 had arms. They decided to reinforce their supporters in the town by raising armed detachments in the countryside. O'Brien led a force which at its greatest strength was to number some 2,000 men on a march that took them to Carrick, Mullinahone, Callan, Killenaule and finally on 26 July to Ballingarry. Here the rebellion finally collapsed after a skirmish with armed police occupying the Widow McCormick's cottage. The rebel force dispersed and its leaders took flight.

Two related questions arise here. First of all, was there any serious prospect of rebellion in an Ireland devastated by hunger and disease; and second, to what extent was O'Brien's leadership responsible for the nature of the final outcome? We have already considered the situation in Dublin, where the best opportunity for a rising had arguably passed with Mitchel's deportation, but what of rural Ireland? Were the small farmers, cottiers and labourers too wasted by famine to take up arms against the British?

Obviously the Famine had had a tremendous impact on these groups, seriously weakening them through death, eviction and emigration and leaving many of the survivors demoralised, apathetic and too malnourished to think of resistance. From this point of view it can be argued that the Famine actually saved Ireland for the British. If the crisis circumstances of 1848 had arisen at a time when the Irish people had been fed and healthy, then, inspired by the French example, they would have posed a sufficient threat either to have extracted substantial concessions from the British or to have plunged the country into rebellion. But what of the conditions that did actually obtain in 1848? Realistically, it seems most unlikely that there could have been a successful rebellion: the British were too strong and determined and the Confederates were too weak and their leadership too indecisive. There was, however, every prospect of a serious outbreak that would have constituted some sort of armed assault on British rule even if it had little or no prospect of success. Even such a defeat would probably have forced the British to introduce a programme of reforms such as were to follow the defeat of the Fenians in 1867.

What evidence is there for concluding that a serious outbreak was possible? First, it is clear that throughout the Famine the small farmers and labourers continued to offer active resistance to the landlords and the British. There was a dramatic rise in agrarian crime, crime aimed overwhelmingly at holding on to the land and carried out by the secret societies that were endemic to the Irish countryside. Whereas in 1843 there were 5,875 agrarian outrages reported, by 1847 the number had increased to 10,986 and it remained high in the following years: 14,980 in 1848 and 14,908 in 1849. The Confederates completely failed to organise this resistance, looking to the Catholic clergy rather than to the secret societies, the Whiteboys and the Ribbonmen, for help in raising the rural districts. While the Famine had certainly ravaged the Irish poor, there was still the potential for armed resistance. This is also borne out by the often wildly enthusiastic reception that the Confederate leaders met with during their short time in the field. Meagher provides a positively surreal description of what met them in Carrick on 24 July:

> A torrent of human beings, rushing through lanes and narrow streets; surging and boiling against the white basements that hemmed it in; whirling in dizzy circles, and tossing up its dark waves, with sounds of wrath, vengeance, and defiance; clenched hands, darting high above the black and broken surface, and waving to and fro, with the wildest confusion in the air; eyes red with rage and desperation, starting and flashing upwards through the billows of the flood; long tresses of hair – disordered, drenched and tangled – streaming in the roaring wind of voices, and, as in a shipwreck, rising and falling with the foam; wild, half-stifled, passionate, frantic prayers of hope; invocations in sobs, and thrilling wailings, and piercing cries, to the God of Heaven, His Saints, and the Virgin Mary; challenges to the foe; curses on the red flag; scornful, exulting, delirious defiances of death.

This was, he concludes 'the Revolution, if we had accepted it'. He then goes on: 'Why it was not accepted I cannot with sufficient accuracy explain ... I remember nothing clearly, save the passion, the confusion and the tumult.'[10] Clearly some sort of determined stand was possible in Carrick. Confederate strength in the town stood at some 3,000 men and John O'Mahony was raising thousands more in the surrounding countryside. He was to bring them into the town, only to find that O'Brien had already moved on. Why was the attempt not made? This brings us to the question of O'Brien's leadership.

William Smith O'Brien had only embarked on the road to rebellion with the greatest reluctance. His heart was never in the enterprise, and whenever the opportunity arose to put off making a stand it was gratefully seized upon. Moreover, this was compounded by his almost comical belief in the sanctity of property rights: he refused to allow his followers to cut down trees for barricades, to commandeer food or to trespass on private property on manoeuvres. Whatever enthusiasm there might have been for the Confederate cause, it was soon dissipated by O'Brien's incapacity. In the circumstances, it is hardly surprising that most of those who rallied to his standard soon thought better of it and slipped away home. O'Brien was categorically not a revolutionary leader; he was a constitutional politician who had been forced to place himself at the head of a revolutionary attempt for fear that it should fall into the hands of Mitchel and Lalor. Such a man could never give decisive leadership to such a desperate undertaking.

1848 and the Catholic Church

One interesting feature of the Confederate enterprise in 1848 is the quite remarkable extent to which it placed its faith in the Catholic clergy, relying on them to raise the rural population. According to Charles Gavan Duffy, 'at this time Pius IX still seemed the appointed leader of the nations striving for freedom' and he expected the Irish clergy to follow the Pope's lead. Priests, he believed, 'might make effective soldiers; they had done so in 1643 and in 1798. They had done so in Spain, New Spain and in Belgium.' Moreover, priests did indeed come forward to offer their services. While he was awaiting trial in early July, Duffy was approached by two young priests who offered to take over editorship of The Nation. One was the future Archbishop Croke of Cashel and the other, Father Barry, was to become head of St Patrick's College, Melbourne, Australia. Duffy also received a message from Bishop Maginn of Derry that if the Confederation waited until the autumn, he would join them 'with twenty officers in black uniforms'.[11] One advantage of this clerical involvement, as far as the likes of Duffy were concerned, was that it also guaranteed the rebellion against becoming an attack on the landlords and their property.

Another participant, John O'Mahony, whom we have already met belatedly leading a large armed contingent into Carrick, also wrote of the reliance that was placed on the clergy. In south Tipperary:

> the originators of the movement were priests. They publicly told the people to form clubs, to make pikes and many a one proclaimed from the altar that he would be with the people and lead them on the day of action ... The older priests opposed the movement a little at first, but such was the impetus given to the revolutionary organisations by Mitchel's deportation that their opposition was soon silenced ... Had not the Young Ireland leaders calculated upon the cordial and active support and cooperation of these clerical revolutionists, they never should have attempted to raise the people after the fashion they did. As it was they were the main hinge upon which the whole movement turned.

O'Mahony was later to become the leader of the Fenian Brotherhood in America. The conclusion he drew from his experience of clerical involvement in the 1848 affair was that it would have been better if 'they had never come into it'.[12] When the time came to take the field, the priests either refused to assist or actively opposed attempts to mobilise the people for battle.

The Confederation leadership was to place much of the blame for its failure on the clergy. O'Brien himself, when preparing notes for his trial, came to the conclusion that:

> it was through the instrumentality of the superior order of the Catholic Clergy that the insurrection was suppressed. For my own part I feel convinced that we were defeated, not by the military preparations of Lord Harding or of General MacDonald, not by the system of espionage organised by Lord Clarendon, but by the influences brought into action by the Catholic Clergy. Whatever merit therefore is connected with the repression of our efforts is due chiefly if not solely to the Catholic Hierarchy.[13]

O'Brien still believed that many priests had been sympathetic but that the 'Hierarchy', the bishops, had prevented their involvement. Duffy came to a similar conclusion: he believed that had the clergy helped the rebellion 'it would have been widespread and protracted', although it was still 'doubtful whether it would have been successful'.[14] As it was, clerical abstention and opposition doomed the attempt. The belief that the clergy were to blame for the Confederate failure was to become almost an article of faith among the 1848 rebels and later the Fenians.

O'Brien's failure was not the end of the matter, however. Armed bands of rebels remained at large on the Tipperary–Kilkenny border and in September 1848 attacked the Glenbower police barracks before dispersing. More significant was the establishment of a network of secret clubs – the Irish Democratic Association – that extended from Dublin to Cork and into the disturbed counties of Kilkenny, Waterford and Tipperary. Lalor was among the instigators of this conspiracy, together with a number of young men who were later to become leading Fenians: John O'Leary, Philip Grey and Thomas Clarke Luby. They flirted with the idea of kidnapping Queen Victoria during her visit to Dublin in August 1849 and laid plans for another rising, but the organisation disintegrated following the failure of an attack on the police barracks at Cappoquin in County Waterford in September. Lalor was to die, worn out and demoralised, soon afterwards. While the Irish Democratic Association never constituted a serious threat to the British, its underground methods of organising in many ways prefigured that of the Fenians.

The revolutionary movement in Ireland had been decisively defeated.

John Mitchel and Irish Republicanism

While Ireland at the end of 1848 was securely under British control and the Confederate rebels had been not only defeated, but also to a considerable extent discredited by their failure to mount a serious challenge, the cause of the Irish Republic still remained very much alive. It was carried across the Atlantic to the United States by the Irish who had fled the Famine and it was to be given voice by John Mitchel. It was to Mitchel that A.M. Sullivan gave the credit, or perhaps the blame, for having 'revived the Separatist or revolutionary party in Irish politics' in 1848.[15] Mitchel was to provide the indictment that was to become the very core of republican ideology and was to rescue the cause from the O'Brien fiasco. He argued in rhetoric of compelling power that the British government had deliberately starved the Irish people in order to safeguard its continued rule over the country. We shall consider the validity of this indictment below; whatever conclusions are drawn in this respect, however, it is still necessary to acknowledge the part that it played in sustaining the republican tradition, not just into the 1860s but up to the present day.

The very day, 27 May 1848, that he was rushed, in chains, out of Ireland, Mitchel began his *Jail Journal*, one of the most remarkable literary works of the nineteenth century. In its pages, he was to declare his hatred not just of the British Empire, 'the Carthaginian sea-monster', but of the very civilisation of which it was the embodiment: nineteenth-century commercial civilisation. He saw Britain as the standard-bearer of free trade and market forces that threatened the dissolution of all social institutions, of all social obligations. While Mitchel, initially a conservative nationalist, had been radicalised by the Famine, his critique of British 'progress' always remained at heart conservative. He looked back to a mythical past when sturdy, independent, small farmers, beholden to no one, had prospered in Ireland. This was his particular utopia. Eventually this conservatism was to corrode his radicalism, yet he remained committed not just to the cause of an Irish Republic, but to the Chartist alliance and to European revolution well into the 1850s.

In his *Journal*, Mitchel mourned the defeat of the revolutionary movements in Germany, Hungary and Italy: 'Kings and Grand Dukes are everywhere rampant – for the present'. With a typically defiant flourish, he asked:

> Has the people's blood then been shed in vain? By God, no! The blood of men fighting for freedom is never shed in vain – the earth will not cover it – from the ground it cries aloud, and the avenger knoweth his day and the hour.

He looked forward to the time when 'the Cypress branch of Young Italy will be reared again' and praised that 'good and noble Italian Mazzini'. His generous sympathies did not, however, extend as far as the 'Red Republicans and Communists' who in June 1848 had risen in Paris: for these 'wild beasts', he believed that 'grape and canister' were the only answer.

The most celebrated section of the *Journal* is the debate between himself, the Ego, and his sceptical other, the Doppelganger. Here he argued out his beliefs and motivations. The dialogue is unique in revolutionary literature. To the charge that his only motivation was hatred of Britain, Mitchel replied by making a distinction between 'the British nation' and 'what Cobbet called the Thing', the British Establishment that oppressed the British people as much as it did the subject peoples. According to Mitchel, the best friend of the British people 'is simply he who approves himself the bitterest enemy of their government and all their institutions'. To the charge that he gloried in bloodshed, he replied by asking his Doppelganger to 'dwell a moment on the horrors of peaceful and constitutional famine'. Which was worse, famine or a war of national liberation? He proclaimed 'the revolutionary Leveller ... your only architect' and called for unrelenting war on 'greedy tyranny (constitutional or other) grinding the faces of the poor'. For Mitchel, 'sansculottism will bring forth venerable institutions'.[16]

Explaining the Famine

Mitchel's most important contribution to the republican cause, however, was his proclaimed belief that the Great Famine was no natural catastrophe, but a crime almost beyond belief. The British, he argued, had taken advantage of the potato blight deliberately to starve the Irish into submission. The problem confronting the British government 'was how to get rid of the people ... to thin out these multitudinous Celts'. While O'Connell had backed down from confrontation at Clontarf in 1843, the powerful movement that he had built up showed the potential for resistance that existed in Ireland. The government had to destroy that potential, and starvation and eviction were its chosen methods. In his *History of Ireland*, Mitchel compared this attempt to complete the conquest of Ireland with an earlier episode:

> In the summer of this year, 1847, Lord Clarendon was sent over as Lord Lieutenant to finish the conquest of Ireland – just as Lord Mountjoy had been sent to bring to an end the wars of Queen Elizabeth's reign – that is by the corruption of the rich and the starvation of the poor. The form of procedure, indeed, was somewhat different; for English statesmen of the sixteenth century had not learned to use the weapons of 'amelioration' and 'political economy'; neither had they yet established the policy of keeping Ireland as a store farm to raise wealth for England. Lord Mountjoy's system, then, had somewhat of a rude character; and he could think of nothing better than sending large bodies of troops to cut down the grass corn, and burn the houses ... Lord Clarendon's method was more in the spirit of the nineteenth century, though his slaughters were more terrible in the end than Lord Mountjoy's. Again there was growing upon Irish soil a noble harvest; but it had been more economical to carry it over to England by help of free trade than to burn it on the ground.

Mitchel argued quite simply that while the potato crop might have failed, there was still more than enough food produced in the country to feed a population twice as great, but this food was exported to England. He wrote of mothers, driven mad, who 'began to eat their young who died of famine before them; and still fleets of ships were sailing with every tide, carrying Irish cattle and corn to England'. This was what 'commerce and free trade did for Ireland in those days'.[17] Michel's indictment, voicing as it did the conviction of many Irish people, both those who stayed and those who fled, became the core of the republican case against British rule.

How valid is Mitchel's case? In one crucial respect, he was clearly wrong: there was a very real food deficit in Ireland during the Famine and it is just not true to say that the whole population could have been fed if it were not for the export of grain. Indeed, the figures show that when starvation was at its worst, more food was imported into the country than was carried out, and still people starved. What is undoubtedly true, however, is that the prohibition of food exports would have saved tens, perhaps hundreds of thousands, of lives. Moreover, the spectacle of armed soldiers guarding convoys carrying grain out of the country from the starving poor still remains incredible. Similarly, the mass evictions carried out with government support throughout the Famine almost defy belief. Only a government that had no need for popular endorsement could have behaved in this way. But was this a policy of deliberate starvation? Once again the evidence does not support his allegation. What is true, however, is that the lives of the Irish poor were not important enough to the British government for it to take the necessary emergency measures, regardless of free trade and market forces, to keep them alive. From this point of view, Mitchel was clearly right that a crime had been committed, but he presented a mistaken indictment.

Whatever the validity of Mitchel's case, his powerful indictment of British imperialism was to be an important component in the development of republican ideology into the 1860s. His ferocious hostility to the British Empire inspired many of those who were to rally to the Fenian movement and steeled them for a resort to arms. For these young men, British rule was forever condemned because of what had happened in the grim years of hunger and mass starvation.

CHAPTER 2

The Fenian Movement

America

The failure of the revolutionary attempts of 1848 and 1849 saw many Irish revolutionaries seek safety in flight to America. It was here that the republican movement was to regroup and from here that the initiative was to come to begin organising again in Ireland. An important impetus was given to these developments by John Mitchel's escape from Van Dieman's Land in July 1853. He arrived in America on 9 October and established himself in New York. Here he started his own newspaper, the *Citizen*, and became actively involved with an exile revolutionary organisation, the Irishmen's Civil and Military Republican Union. Other veterans of the 1848 rising, most notably John O'Mahony and Michael Doheny, were also involved. They hoped for a renewal of the European revolutions that would inevitably engulf Britain and Ireland, and tried to prepare the New York Irish for the coming struggle. In the *Citizen's* first issue, which appeared on 7 January 1854, Mitchel proclaimed that the 'movement of all the Western and Southern nations of Europe is towards Republicanism ... Europe is again ripening fast for another bursting forth of the precious and deathless spirit of freedom.' He looked to the British working-class for allies, 'men voteless, landless, rightless, who labour for ever in mines and factories' and who had 'no interest in the oppression of Ireland, in the plunder of Asia'. Somewhat optimistically, Mitchel and his colleagues believed that the Crimean War of 1854–6 presaged a fresh revolutionary outbreak and began preparations for an armed expedition to raise the standard of revolt in Ireland once again. They despatched Joseph Denieffe back across the Atlantic to reorganise the revolutionary movement and make ready for the day.

Nothing came of this enterprise, however, and instead Mitchel found himself embroiled in two disputes that in many ways exemplify the contradictory character of his politics. His public support for the Italian revolutionary movement led to a bitter quarrel with the Catholic Church in New York, a quarrel made all the more fierce by his belief that the priests had betrayed the Confederate cause in 1848. At the same time, his equally public support for black slavery brought him into conflict with New York's Abolitionist movement.

22

Over the course of the next decade, Mitchel's support for European revolution was to atrophy while his enthusiasm for black slavery came to rival his commitment to an Irish Republic. Indeed, he was actually to argue that black slavery should be introduced into the Irish Republic once it was established. His racism was to blind him to the nature of one of the most vicious and oppressive regimes of the time and make him its defender. Despairing of the Irish cause, Mitchel left New York for Tennessee and the South, where he was to make a name for himself as a pro-slavery newspaper editor. Only after the South's defeat in the Civil War was he to rally once again to the Irish Republican cause.

While Mitchel withdrew, at least temporarily, from the struggle for an Irish Republic, O'Mahony, Doheny and others continued their efforts. They disbanded the Irishmen's Civil and Military Republican Union in favour of the more innocent-sounding Emmet Monument Association, but their objectives remained the same. They hoped to use America as a secure base from which to rebuild the revolutionary movement in Ireland, ready for when Britain was embroiled in foreign war and from where an armed expedition could be despatched once rebellion had broken out. The man they chose to be their agent in Ireland was James Stephens.

James Stephens and the IRB

Among the participants in the 1848 and 1849 risings were many of the men who were later to be among the founders and instigators of the Fenian movement. The most remarkable of these was without doubt James Stephens, who had been with Smith O'Brien at Ballingarry before fleeing the country to avoid arrest. Stephens escaped to France, where he remained, living in comparative poverty, for a number of years. Here he became involved in the revolutionary underground, in the secret societies and clubs that had survived the defeat of the June 1848 insurrection in Paris and later of the revolutionary movement throughout Europe. He lived alongside revolutionary exiles from all over Europe and, according to his own testimony, was to fight with them on the barricades when Louis Napoleon staged his coup d'état in December 1851. Much later, he was to recall that during his time in Paris he had been particularly impressed by the exiled Italian revolutionaries he had met, 'for the Italians have in a certain way perfected conspiracy, and I thought that with certain reserves they were the methods to follow'. How far the Fenian movement was to derive from a native Irish tradition of underground revolutionary organisation, the Ribbon tradition, and how far from Continental models is an interesting point. Certainly Irish revolutionaries had learned the need for secrecy in 1848, and the 1849 movement had operated under-ground. Nevertheless Fenian organisation, with its circles and centres, does seem to have borrowed from the European experience. It is perhaps best in this regard to see Stephens and others as grafting aspects of the European revolutionary tradition on to the native Irish.

While in his French exile, Stephens was converted from narrow nationalist views to a socialist and internationalist perspective. He wrote in his diary in January 1859:

> I would fight for an abstract principle of right in defence of any country; and were England a republic battling for human freedom on the one hand, and Ireland leagued with despots on the other, I should, unhesitatingly, take up arms against my native land. In a word, the only countries I recognize over the earth are Toil and Privilege; the one of these I shall struggle for, the other against, with all the faculties of my being.

While he saw the struggle for an Irish Republic as an integral part of a broader international conflict embracing as allies both the British working-class and the European revolutionary movement, many other Fenians were to remain narrow nationalists and even, as in John Mitchel's case, became positively reactionary on various issues.

Stephens eventually returned to Ireland early in 1856 with the intention of assessing the possibility of a revival of revolutionary activity. He toured the country on foot, meeting hundreds of sympathisers, many of them veterans of 1848 and 1849, and concluded both that the attempt was possible and that it was urgently needed. He found, in his own words, that Ireland 'was politically dead ... that she had given up the ghost, and was at last, to all intents and purposes, one of England's reconquered provinces'.[1]

Nevertheless Stephens was so confident of his ability to establish a revolutionary underground that he sent Joseph Denieffe back to New York, promising to raise 10,000 men within three months if the American organisation could provide a subsidy of £100 a month. This in turn was enthusiastically agreed, but in practice it was to prove impossible to raise the necessary funds to pay the subsidy. By the time Stephens came to establish the Irish Revolutionary Brotherhood (IRB) in Peter Langan's woodyard in Dublin on 17 March 1858, St Patrick's Day, he had only received a fraction of what he had been promised. This failure on the part of the American exiles was continually to compromise the effort in Ireland. While founded as the Irish Revolutionary Brotherhood, the IRB soon became the Irish Republican Brotherhood, but it was to be more generally known as the Fenian movement.

The IRB was to be an oath-bound secret society, organised into circles, each with some 800 members commanded by a centre or 'A'. Under each 'A' were nine 'B's or captains, each commanding some 90 men, and under each 'B' were nine 'C's or sergeants, each commanding nine men. The intention was that each individual member of the organisation would only know his immediate comrades and his immediate superior. This, it was hoped, would prevent penetration by spies and informers. In practice, the structure was to break down as recruits poured in, and the organisation became much more open than was intended. Circles increased in size, sometimes into the thousands, and members knew other members outside their own unit. Although generally portrayed as a symptom of the organisation's failure, this can more appropriately be seen as a consequence of its success. The circle or 'cellular' system of organisation was appropriate for a small tightly knit secret society, but not for the mass movement that Fenianism was to become. Nevertheless, while its structure did not prove a successful barrier to spies and informers, especially those among the leadership, what is more creditable is the movement's success in surviving repression and defeat. The IRB was not to be destroyed by the mass arrests of 1865–7 or by the failure of the 1867 rising, but survived into the 1870s, up to 1916 and after, only finally dissolving in 1924. This certainly tends to support the view that Stephens, whatever his other weaknesses, was an effective organiser. He was to exercise an autocratic control over the organisation until he was overthrown at the end of 1866.

The new organisation began to recruit, only slowly at first, but this was to be expected. Stephens and his chief lieutenant, Thomas Clarke Luby, travelled the country, recruiting organisers and establishing IRB circles. This was difficult work at which Stephens excelled. His most notable success came in May 1858, when he succeeded in recruiting Jeremiah O'Donovon Rossa and his Phoenix Society of Skibbereen, County Cork, into the organisation. An underground network was established that gradually came to extend over most of the country, with the only exception being the Protestant north.

Central to Stephen's revolutionary strategy at this time were the beliefs, first, that the IRB must be prepared to take advantage of British involvement in foreign wars, and, second, that it must ally itself with the British labour movement. Foreign war, it was believed, would empty Ireland of troops and make a successful rising possible. The Crimean War had earlier seemed to present such an opportunity, the Indian 'Mutiny' of 1857 had been looked to, and then in the years from 1858 to 1860 there was great hope that war would break out between Britain and France, a war it was believed the French would win. By early 1861, however, it was clear that the

Anglo-French crisis was over and that relations were improving. The other side of the strategy, the British alliance, relied on a revival of Radicalism, of the Chartist spirit as Stephens termed it. His hopes in this regard were not to be met until the Reform agitation of the mid-1860s. Meanwhile, the IRB continued to organise, waiting for the day.

The unreliability of the American exiles was still a problem. In October 1858 Stephens travelled to New York with the intention of bringing them into line with the IRB. He set about energetically raising funds and imposed a reorganisation of the American wing of the movement, installing John O'Mahony as Head Centre of the newly formed Fenian Brotherhood. O'Mahony, a classical scholar, took the name from the Fianna, the bodyguard of the legendary Gaelic warrior, Fiona MacCumhail. 'Fenian' was, in fact, to become the generic name for Irish revolutionaries in both Ireland and America. After a remarkably successful visit, Stephens returned to Ireland in March 1859.

Stephens regarded the moderate nationalists who were vainly attempting to rebuild a constitutional nationalist movement to succeed O'Connell's long defunct Repeal movement with particular hostility. They were potential rivals whose influence, such as it was, had to be destroyed. He was especially concerned to counter the efforts of A.M. Sullivan, the then editor of *The Nation* newspaper and one of the key figures in the constitutional nationalist enterprise. His tactic was quite simple: when Sullivan criticised the revived activities of the revolutionary underground, he was accused of 'felon setting', of betraying the organisation to the authorities. This accusation was intended both to discredit the moderates and to deter them from further criticism. Sullivan was himself to make a number of appeals to the physical-force tradition in *The Nation* at this time, but this was really only an attempt to compete with the IRB for support, an attempt that was to fail.

The McManus Funeral

The conflict with the moderate nationalists came to a head over the McManus funeral affair of 1861. Terence Bellew McManus had been a leading Confederate in Liverpool and in 1848 had crossed to Ireland to join Smith O'Brien's attempted rising. He had been captured and was transported to Van Dieman's Land, only to escape to America, where he settled in San Francisco. McManus died after an accident on 14 January 1861 and was buried without much fuss two days later. No sooner had the body been interred than the Fenian Brotherhood in San Francisco began a campaign to ship his remains back to Ireland. Eventually, in August, the body was exhumed, placed in a metal coffin inside a rosewood casket and shipped to New York. Here a Fenian committee, led by Thomas Francis Meagher, waited on Archbishop Hughes to request a Solemn High Requiem Mass. Not only did Hughes agree, but his own address to the congregation proclaimed that 'there are cases in which it is lawful to resist and overthrow a tyrannical government'.[2] While he undoubtedly intended these remarks to apply to the 1848 rising, the Fenians were to seize on them as a clerical vindication of their activities. The remains finally left New York for Ireland on 19 October, arriving on the 30th.

It is likely that Michael Doheny and John O'Mahony hoped to use the McManus funeral as the signal for a rising. Stephens, however, was well aware of the impracticality of such a proposition. Although the IRB was growing in strength, it had pitifully few arms and limited funds. Instead, he intended to use the occasion to strengthen the organisation, recruiting new members and extending its influence. He made use of the recently established National Brotherhood of St Patrick, a loose association of open and legal nationalist clubs, that served as a front for the IRB's activities. This precipitated a bitter struggle with the surviving leaders of the 1848 rising, Smith O'Brien, John Dillon, John Martin, Father Kenyon and others, all of whom were now hostile to revolutionary organisation and embraced constitutional methods. They were comprehensively outmanoeuvred.

The McManus funeral also brought the IRB into open conflict with the Catholic Church in Ireland. This had already occurred at a local level, but now the Fenians confronted Archbishop, later to become Cardinal, Cullen of Dublin, the most powerful man in the Irish Church. Unlike Archbishop Hughes in New York, the Irish hierarchy, with only a few exceptions, refused to countenance the funeral. In Cork, Bishop Delaney would not allow the remains to lie in any of his churches. Despite this clerical disapproval, a large determined procession followed the coffin through the city. Similarly in Dublin, Archbishop Cullen would not allow the use of any of the city's churches and forbade any of his priests to officiate at the funeral. Nevertheless, perhaps as many as 50,000 people followed the coffin through Dublin on 10 December. This impressive demonstration was marshalled by John O'Clohissey, a former British soldier, president of the Dublin Trades Council and a Fenian centre. The IRB had triumphed in the face of moderate nationalist rivalry and clerical opposition. More members, it was later claimed, were recruited into the organisation during the three weeks that the remains were in Ireland than in the previous two years. The IRB, hitherto weak in Dublin, was now firmly established among the city's working-class. Stephens' strategy was bearing fruit: the IRB was becoming a force in the land.

The Irish People

One of the more surprising steps for an underground organisation to take was the establishment of its own newspaper, the *Irish People*, in November 1863. This was partly intended as a fundraising enterprise: the IRB was still only receiving small and irregular sums from America and Stephens hoped to be able to subsidise its activities and preparations from the expected profits. It was also hoped that having a newspaper under its own control would help consolidate the movement's influence. This has often been portrayed as being at odds with the IRB's secret activities, but really this misunderstands the character of the rising that Stephens and his comrades were working towards. They were not planning a coup d'état to be carried out by a small tightly knit organisation of conspirators, but rather for a popular rebellion that would put large forces into the field capable of waging a war of liberation against the British. Such an enterprise required both the building of a secret revolutionary organisation and the creation of a sympathetic popular opinion. The *Irish People* was intended to serve both these ends.

Against this, it can be argued that the open publication of a legal newspaper made the movement too visible and consequently too vulnerable to British repression. There was some truth in this, but it had to be weighed against other considerations: the rallying of popular support was regarded both as necessary for a successful rising and as the best protection against the British. It is, moreover, important to remember that when the British did finally move against the movement, suppressing the *Irish People* and rounding up those producing it, the organisation itself survived and continued to pose a serious threat. The paper never, of course, made a profit.

The *Irish People* not only rallied the IRB's members and sympathisers, it also served to paralyse the movement's more moderate constitutional opponents. In this capacity, it played a key role in the Fenians' domination of Irish politics in the 1860s. The decisive clash with the constitutional nationalists came on 22 February 1864 when A.M. Sullivan and others organised a public meeting at the Dublin Rotundo to protest against the proposed erection of a statue of Prince Albert on College Green. The meeting was disrupted and taken over by IRB supporters who drove off the platform speakers after fighting had broken out on the floor. This brought home quite forcefully that the constitutional nationalists did not at this time have the necessary support even to hold public meetings in the capital. What followed was an even more dramatic demonstration of their weakness. Some moderates, among them John Blake Dillon, the former Young Irelander, turned to the Catholic Church for support against the Fenians. They succeeded in enlisting the help of the hierarchy, most notably Archbishop

Cullen. In December 1864, a handpicked and carefully policed meeting, once again in the Rotundo, launched the National Association of Ireland as a rival to Fenianism. The new organisation's political timidity and reliance on clerical support was such that even many constitutional nationalists kept their distance. It was never to pose any threat to the IRB.

Who Were the Fenians?

What was the character of the organisation that Stephens and his comrades were building? It was a revolutionary organisation committed to the staging of an armed rebellion against British rule and to the establishment of an Irish Republic. But who were the men who joined it and rallied to its cause? The starting point for any discussion of the nature of the IRB has to be its social composition.

According to Stephens, the IRB recruited 'the farmers' sons, the mechanics, the artisans, the labourers and small shopkeepers'. In this respect it was, he asserted, 'wholly and unequivocally democratic'. The evidence we have supports his contention. While the movement's membership was overwhelmingly working-class, its leadership in the main came from the lower middle class. Nevertheless, these men were leading a movement with a democratic social composition. One of the best guides to the IRB's social composition is provided by the occupational background of the 1,100 men arrested between 1866 and 1868 under the Habeas Corpus Suspension Act. Of these, no less than 47.8 per cent (520) were artisans or skilled workers, 6.4 per cent (69) town labourers and 5.3 per cent (58) farm labourers, while another 9.1 per cent (99) were clerks or schoolteachers and 3.6 per cent (39) were shop assistants. Another snapshot, this time of those actually arrested in March 1867 for taking part in the rising, gives us 7 tailors, 1 gas fitter, 1 engine fitter, 3 boot- and shoemakers, 1 plasterer, 1 car driver, 2 engine drivers, 1 coachmaker, 3 nailers, 6 labourers, 3 coopers, 3 ironworkers, 1 tobacco spinner, 1 smith, 2 grocers, 1 letter carrier, 2 messengers, 3 medical students, 1 shop assistant, 1 stationer, 1 brushmaker, 2 millers, 1 baker, 4 drapers, 1 draper's assistant, 1 rectifying distiller, 5 porters, 2 clerks, 1 cabinet maker, 1 ropemaker, 1 mason, 1 bricklayer, 1 plumber, 3 carpenters, 2 slaters, 1 weaver, 1 dyer, 2 stonecutters, 3 corkcutters, 1 printer and 1 painter. The skilled trades were nearly all represented. Similarly, if we look at the 62 Fenian prisoners held on board the *Hougoment*, the last ship to carry convicts to Australia, which sailed from London in October 1867, we find they included 10 labourers, 8 clerks, 2 schoolteachers, a journalist, a soldier and some 30 members of the skilled trades. Admittedly these are different snapshots of the same men, that is of those arrested by the British, but nevertheless it is clear that the IRB was a working-class organisation and more particularly that it was rooted in the skilled working-class, among the artisans. If we take into account Fenian success at recruiting in the army, this almost certainly increases the proportion of labourers in the movement, but the general conclusion still stands. Much more work needs to be done on the artisan culture and politics of Dublin and other towns in this period before we have an adequate account of Fenianism's social character, of the lives of those men who made it a mass movement.[3] What we can discuss here, however, are the consequences of its social composition.

It has long been customary to regard the Fenian movement in the 1860s as having been agnostic on social questions. While Stephens held advanced radical views, he did not proselytise for them within the IRB or try to secure their adoption as the organisation's programme. With regard to the land question in particular, it has been argued that the Fenians missed the opportunity to raise the countryside against the British by failing to follow James Fintan Lalor's advice and launch a land agitation. Michael Davitt, himself a Fenian activist in the 1860s and later one of the architects of the Land War of the 1880s, harshly blamed Fenianism for giving 'the landlords of Ireland almost twenty years of agrarian peace'. Indeed, Stephens himself boasted that 'we crushed Ribbonism wherever it predominated ... during the period that Fenianism was an all-powerful factor in the politics of the country, never was the country freer from the strains of agrarian crime'. He made clear elsewhere his personal view of 'the comparative worthlessness of separation without the abolition of landlordism', but argued that he 'did not think it possible at the time to inaugurate a land movement ... and, moreover, I found the labourers and mechanics would never join the tenantry shoulder to shoulder in the enterprise'.[4]

This raises a number of points. First of all, Davitt's censure is much too harsh. The comparative agrarian peace of the 1860s had socioeconomic causes rather than deriving from the politics of Fenianism, and was moreover one of the factors contributing to the weakness of constitutional nationalism during this period. More to the point is Stephens' observation that the artisans and labourers were not prepared to ally themselves with the large tenant-farmers, with the rural middle class. This reluctance was fully reciprocated.

Why was this? It is not in fact true that the IRB had nothing to say about the land question. While it was not the organisation's central concern, the Fenian newspaper, the *Irish People*, did proclaim that the land belonged to the people. The 'people', however, was a much broader and more democratic category than was acceptable to the large tenant-farmers, the beneficiaries of the Famine clearances, who were convinced that the land was rightfully theirs. This social group had, as we have already seen, dramatically increased in social weight, in numbers and wealth, as a consequence of the Famine, and by the 1860s it was in the process of trying to consolidate its position as the dominant social group among the Catholic population. Now its members found this position challenged and themselves under attack. The 'people', according to the Fenian interpretation of the word, included the rural working-class and even those who had been driven from the land by hunger and disease in the 1840s. This was directly subversive of the social interests and ambitions of the large tenant-farmers. Moreover, the *Irish People* attacked them for their lack of national spirit, their selfishness and their greed. This was music to the ears of the movement's working-class supporters, but was obviously symptomatic of the tensions and conflicts that existed between the farmers and the working class, rather than providing any basis for an alliance between them. The large tenant-farmers were, in this period, to prove themselves the enemies of Fenianism, not so much because they had moral objections to physical force, although revolution was often seen as a threat to both Catholic and Protestant property, but because they were opposed to and felt threatened by the independent political organisation of people they considered their social inferiors, members of a subordinate class. The Catholic middle classes, in both town and country, regarded the Fenian movement as a democratic threat to their domination of the Catholic population. Their hostility was, as we shall see, to be given voice not by constitutional nation-alists (who were too weak to undertake the task at this time), but by the Catholic Church.

Despite its concerns with secrecy and underground organisation, as Fenianism developed into a mass movement its members came increasingly to conduct themselves in public in ways that were seen to challenge authority and the social order. The Fenians who met together at fairs, in public houses and other social gatherings were looked on, according to one historian:

> as posing a social threat by becoming openly assertive towards the authorities. In other words, they were losing the 'tug-of-the-forelock' mentality that traditionally pervaded Irish society. The Fenians came mainly from the lower classes – artisans, town and country labourers, small farmers. Some of them, at least instinctively, resented the place delegated to them in Irish society by their social betters ... Lack of deference became almost a physical characteristic in the eyes of the authorities.[5]

This is an important point. While Fenianism did not have a social revolutionary programme, its very existence as a working-class revolutionary organisation inevitably challenged the position and authority of the Protestant ascendancy, the British and, of course, the Catholic middle class. This challenge was evident even in the bearing of the young men who had been sworn into the conspiracy: deference was replaced by defiance, the bowed head by the insolent stare. It remained an implicit aspect of Fenian politics rather than becoming an explicit stance, an aspect of the class-in-itself rather than of the class-for-itself, but nevertheless it was one of the Fenian movement's defining features. For the Fenians, class was always to be subsumed by nation, but, as we have seen, their nationalism was inevitably informed by their experience of class and class relations. The IRB of the 1860s was not to develop beyond being a revolutionary democratic movement into a revolutionary socialist movement, despite its working-class composition, its commitment to armed insurrection and the radicalism of many of its leaders and much of its rank and file. Indeed, mass support for socialist politics would have to wait in Ireland for the rise of 'Larkinism', of James Larkin, James Connolly and the Irish Transport and General Workers Union, in the years immediately before the First World War.

The Fenians and the Church

'We meant to kill clerical dictation, and we did kill it' was the large claim made by John O'Leary in his celebrated *Recollections of Fenians and Fenianism*. And this claim has been accepted at face value by many later historians. The reality is somewhat more complex, not least because while the Fenian movement did indeed defy the censures of the Church, its members nevertheless overwhelmingly remained devout Catholics. The Church's hostility to revolution did not, in Ireland, produce the ferocious anti-clericalism that was to characterise revolutionary movements on the Continent throughout the nineteenth and into the twentieth centuries.

While the IRB had from its inception in 1858 been determined to organise independently of the clergy and to place no reliance on their support, this still did not involve either a rejection of Catholicism or any assault upon the position of the Church in Irish society. Once again according to O'Leary, the IRB had seen from the very beginning that 'ecclesiastical authority in temporal affairs should be shivered to atoms before we could advance a single step towards the liberation of our struggling country'. Not only was he exaggerating the movement's consistency in this endeavour; even if his statement is taken as valid, this did not amount to an anti-clerical assault on the Church as such, but was restricted to the smaller target of 'the priest-in-politics'.[6] There is, moreover, some evidence to suggest that the objection was not so much to clerical intervention in politics in principle, as to clerical intervention against the IRB.

The McManus funeral is quite interesting in this regard. While the affair brought the movement into conflict with the hierarchy, this was primarily because it was recognised at least in part as an attempt to get the Church to endorse the politics of revolutionary separatism. The funeral organisers had requested that Archbishop Cullen should allow the remains to lie in state in Dublin's cathedral and that he should perform a grand religious ceremonial over them. This was hardly the action of principled anti-clericals and is in stark contrast to the militantly secular funerals that were to be a feature of European democratic and revolutionary movements. It was Cullen's steadfast refusal that was the cause of contention. Moreover, the Church was not united in its hostility. Much to the satisfaction of the Fenians, Bishop Keane of Cloyne allowed the remains to lie in a church in Queenstown, students at Maynooth College held a Requiem Office for McManus as a gesture of solidarity, and a number of priests defied Cullen by attending the funeral. One republican priest, Father Lavelle of Partry, delivered a provocative oration over the grave, warning the mourners that the day of independence 'for which our fathers yearned, struggled, fought and suffered cannot now be far off'.[7] These were very much exceptions to general clerical hostility, but they nevertheless show that the Fenians did in fact welcome clerical support when it was forthcoming. Indeed, far from their hostility to the priest-in-politics being a principled position, it can be more accurately seen as a reaction to the censure of the movement orchestrated by Archbishop Cullen. The IRB was, as we have already seen, committed to organising independently of the clergy, but the campaign against the priest-in-politics that was to be waged in the *Irish People* in no way derived from this position. Rather it has to be seen as the response by a movement made up overwhelmingly of men who remained staunch Catholics, to the vigour with which the Church opposed and condemned their activities.

While the pages of the *Irish People* carried numerous attacks on priests who opposed the movement, there were strict limits to this anti-clericalism. The paper was edited by John O'Leary, a lapsed Catholic, closely assisted by Luby, a Protestant, but its editorials condemning clerical intervention in politics were written by Charles Kickham, who always remained a devout Catholic. As Kickham himself insisted: 'We never uttered a word against the priests as ministers of religion. But we challenged and do challenge their right to dictate to the people in politics.'[8] Another frequent scourge of the clergy in the paper's columns was James F.X. O'Brien, another staunch Catholic, who wrote under the pseudonym of 'De l'Abbaye'. Two of O'Brien's sons were to become priests. This was hardly the stuff of a full-blooded anti-clericalism on the Continental model. It was a much more limited affair. The priests and bishops were attacked for their politics without this in any way calling into question their domination over other areas of Catholic social life. The political stand adopted by the Church was seen as the result of the dominance of pro-British bishops and of British intrigue at the Vatican, rather than as inherent in Catholic doctrine or intrinsic to the nature of the Church. This was made all the more credible by the well-known sympathy, or even supposed sympathy, of individual priests and bishops for the revolutionary cause.

Certainly one of the most significant features of the clash between the Fenians and the Church is the small number of those who actually abandoned their faith. Individuals such as John O'Leary, Jeremiah O'Donovon Rossa, Patrick 'Pagan' O'Leary, Frank Roney and even Stephens himself were very much the exception. Much more typical was the 'sterling piety', in John Denvir's words, of the Fenians who assembled for the attack on Chester Castle in February 1867, who had 'thronged the confessionals on that Saturday night and Sunday morning to make their peace with God, satisfied, if need be, to give their lives for the holy cause of Irish Freedom'. Or the 'crowds of young men', whom Richard Pigott observed in Dublin in March 1867, 'hurrying to the churches to make their peace with God before taking the field'. What other revolutionary movement would, for example, have used the celebration of the consecration of a Catholic church as the occasion for a mobilisation and display of strength? This was precisely what the IRB did in Kilkenny in August 1864. Several thousand Fenians assembled in the town, forming, in the words of John Devoy, a disciplined body among the crowds, so that 'the men were able to see that they had the material for an army and were greatly encouraged'.[9] As far as most Fenians were concerned, this linking together of Catholicism and republicanism was perfectly natural and clerical censure was not enough to call it into question.

Indeed, their devotion to the Catholic faith was such that it drew reluctant recognition even from their most hostile opponents: Edward Manning wrote from England to Archbishop Cullen in early February 1866 that 'Your Grace will be happy to know that the Fenian prisoners in Pentonville have asked for Mass, and the Government has granted it. This is a strange victory, on which I make no comment except "Thank God".' Elsewhere Manning wrote that his heart bled for these men who believed 'themselves to be serving in a sacred and holy war for their country and religion'.[10]

Two distinct issues arise here: first of all, what was the basis for the Catholicism of these Fenian revolutionaries; and second, how did they reconcile their religious beliefs with the censures of the Church? The origin of the continuing Catholicism of Irish revolutionaries can be traced back as far as the Elizabethan conquest and the first manifestation of English rule in Ireland as a specifically Protestant ascendancy. This Protestant complexion of the conquest became more pronounced as time went on, reaching its highpoint in the penal regime that followed the Treaty of Limerick of 1691. Opposition to English rule throughout this period took the form of a Catholic Jacobite reaction. Inevitably Irish nationalism as it emerged in the nineteenth century bore the marks of this long gestation: Catholicism and nationalism were inseparably linked in the consciousness of all classes of the Irish population. Even Jeremiah O'Donovon Rossa, a bitter Fenian opponent of 'the priest-in-politics', nevertheless acknowledged how 'Catholic Irishmen came to feel that in fighting against Protestantism, they were fighting against England, and, in fighting for Catholicity, they were fighting for Ireland.' This, he recalled, was the tradition of his youth, when the parish priest was seen as 'the embodiment of hostility to England'. He regretted that this close relationship had broken down in the 1860s, but blamed this on Archbishop Cullen and his Castle-bishops.[11]

The Hardest Test

It is important to recognise the powerful hold that Catholicism and the Church had on even Irish republicans. This is all the more surprising considering that they acknowledged as the ideological inspiration of their movement Protestant revolutionaries such as Theobald Wolfe Tone and Robert Emmet, and more recently Thomas Davis and John Mitchel. How was this trick accomplished? Individual Protestants were welcomed into the movement, even into leadership positions, as long as their beliefs and actions did not offend or conflict with the Catholic faith of the overwhelming majority of its members. This was not always easy. Those aspects of Tone's writings where he expressed his contempt for Catholic superstition and hoped to see the influence of the Church in Ireland broken were conveniently forgotten in favour of his nonsectarian appeals for national unity. Others, like Mitchel, accepted that they were members of a religious minority in a movement that was defined at least in part by its Catholicism. They certainly did not see themselves as members of a secular movement, but rather as a tolerated minority in a primarily Catholic movement. This would

after all be the Protestant position in the Irish Republic that they
hoped to establish. What success did the Fenians have in recruiting
Protestants? Certainly they made little headway in the north, but
in Dublin there was, according to Devoy, a Fenian circle made up
of Protestant artisans.

The contrast with European revolutionary movements in this
period could not be more dramatic. While the Fenians responded
to clerical condemnation and censure blow for blow, in every other
respect the clergy were treated with all due reverence. This was a
milk-and-water anti-clericalism compared to that of French, Italian
or Spanish revolutionaries. Only in Poland did revolutionaries
define themselves as Catholic in the same way as the Fenians did.
The contrast with the European experience is nowhere more clearly
highlighted than by the Irish response to the Italian Risorgimento.
In 1859–60 the Irish Church mounted a campaign of support for
the Papal States against the encroachments of Piedmont. This
campaign assumed massive proportions and took on something of
the character of a popular crusade. Some 1,000 Irish volunteers
were despatched to fight for the Pope, including a contingent of
Fenians. Such behaviour would have been altogether incompre-
hensible to Italian revolutionaries, to the followers of Mazzini and
Garibaldi. It only becomes comprehensible once the limits of
Fenian anti-clericalism are recognised and the extent of their
Catholicism is appreciated.

How did they reconcile their Catholicism with defiance of the
censures of the Church? According to John Devoy, clerical censure
was 'the hardest test the Fenians had to face'.[12] A devout Catholic
himself, Devoy believed that men such as him were able to confront
this challenge and yet remain within the fold of the Church because
it was not united in its hostility to Fenianism. While the great
majority of the bishops condemned the revolutionaries, it was
widely known that both Archbishop McHale of Tuam and Bishop
Keane of Cloyne had declined to instruct their priests to refuse
absolution to IRB members. When the Papal Rescript explicitly
condemning Fenianism was finally issued in January 1870, neither
of them promulgated it. McHale's supposed partiality towards
Fenianism was common knowledge. He protected Father Lavelle,
the Fenian priest, from Cullen's anger. In April 1864 he even sent
three autographed portraits of himself to be sold at a Fenian Fair
in Chicago.

Many young priests also sympathised, but remained silent for
fear of their bishop. John Mitchel, who was to become increasingly
sceptical about prospects for a successful rising, was nevertheless
comforted by the evidence of rebel sentiments that he encountered
among the younger clergy. Soon after he resigned his post as

Fenian agent in Paris in June 1866, he visited the Irish College and was mobbed by cheering students:

> The scene was, under all the circumstances, a strange and touching one. Most of these fine young fellows had been yet unborn when I left my country in 1848; they could have known me only by the tradition of their various counties, and by such publications of mine as they might meet with. It strikes me that if they cheer me so warmly, they cannot be very earnestly loyal to the British Empire; and next year or the year after, most of these will be curates in towns and country parishes all over Ireland ... What is his Eminence Cardinal Cullen going to do about it? How will he ever make the young priests, educated in this Irish College, good faithful West Britons? And Maynooth, I hear, is no better ... Will he excommunicate them and damn all their souls?[13]

Cullen's position, then, was not as strong as it first appeared. Even in Dublin he was defied: the Jesuits did not refuse the sacraments to Fenians, so that men denied them by their own priest could receive them at Gardiner Street Church. It was this evidence of republican sympathy within the Church that, in Devoy's words, 'largely counteracted the effect of the Cardinal's hostility'.[14] It enabled the Fenians to ascribe clerical censure to political bias and prejudice and to argue that it had nothing to do with religion as such; that it was, in fact, possible to be both a good Catholic and a Fenian.

The Church's View of Fenianism

One last point remains to be considered: why it was that the Church under Cullen was so vehement in its hostility to Fenianism? The traditional view is that Cullen was a 'Castle-bishop', that he was anti-nationalist and pro-British. Certainly, the Fenians denounced him as such, but the reality was quite different.

Cullen had a great antipathy to the British and to Protestants in general, an antipathy that was intensified by British support for the cause of Italian nationalism. This was combined, however, with an even more intense fear of revolution and what he believed to be its certain consequences for the Church in Ireland. He had been in Rome in 1848 and had vivid memories of the revolution that had driven Pius IX from the city:

> I well recollect the dreadful night after Rossi's murder [Rossi was the Roman Prime Minister]: it was a night that was calculated to give some idea of the horrors of the first French Revolution, and to inspire every Christian heart with horror. The perpetrators of that dreadful crime walked in procession

through the streets, waving torches over their heads, yelling in their exultation like demons, and singing in frantic strains the infernal words: 'Blessed the hand that spilt the blood of Rossi'. The following day, the same men, drunk with blood, assailed the Pope's palace, fired into his windows, murdered one of his secretaries, Mgr Palma, and compelled His Holiness to surrender himself into their hands. Had he not, a few days afterwards, providentially escaped from them, in all probability they would have sacrilegiously shed his blood. Soon after the Pope's flight a republic was proclaimed, church property was confiscated, the silver and gold vessels and even the bell, taken from the churches, and many peaceable citizens fell victim to the foul system of assassination.

As far as Cullen was concerned, the Fenian movement was tainted with the same 'revolutionary spirit' as Continental revolutionaries. 'If ever', he warned, 'an attempt is made to abridge the rights and liberties of the Catholic Church in Ireland, it will not be by the English government nor by a 'no-popery' cry in England, but by the revolutionary and irreligious nationalists of Ireland.' He was determined that the Irish Church should not have to undergo the same experience of revolution as the Church in Rome. Even British Protestant rule was preferable to this.[15] His fears were, as we have already seen, misplaced.

Are Cullen's personal fears enough to explain the hostility to the IRB of the great majority of the bishops and priests? Certainly not. In order to understand why it was that the clergy in the main followed his lead with regard to the Fenians, we have to understand the distinctive nature of the Catholic Church in Ireland. Unlike on the Continent, where the Church was either a great landowner or was financed by the state, in Ireland it relied on the donations of its congregation, in the main on the large tenant-farmers. This had important political consequences. On the Continent, the Church acted as an ally of the great landowners, as a supporter of conservative, even reactionary governments. In Ireland, it was the ally and representative of the well-to-do farmers, of the rural middle class. It was these people who formed the core of its congregation, who financed it and who staffed it with their sons and daughters. The bishops and priests by and large shared the economic, social and political values and prejudices of this class, from whom they originated, to whom they were related and on whom they were dependent. When the clergy condemned the Fenians, they did so not because they were pro-British (although some were) or because all secret societies were condemned by the Church (although some did) or even because Cullen wished it, but because they were representing the hostility of the Catholic middle class. Cullen's fears were their fears. This group felt threatened by the Fenians and used its Church to defend itself. There was no national constitutional party at this time that could oppose or contain the revolutionaries, so the task fell primarily to the priests. Later, towards the end of the 1870s and early in the 1880s, when Parnell's constitutional nationalists entered into an uneasy alliance with the IRB, the Church was eventually, in the main, to endorse this 'New Departure', not because of any change in Catholic doctrine, but because it had the support of the large tenant-farmers. The Catholic Church in Ireland had to be seen as representing the interests of the Catholic middle class, and nowhere was this more true than in its hostility to Fenianism.

CHAPTER 3

The Rising

1865: the Year of Missed Opportunity

By early 1865 the IRB had grown into a formidable revolutionary underground that constituted a serious threat to British rule in Ireland. There are no reliable figures for the membership of the organisation; the various claims and estimates made by participants and subsequent commentators vary widely. The movement's most recent historian, R.V. Comerford, grudgingly concedes some tens of thousands, but this seems likely to be a conservative estimate. Stephens himself claimed 80,000 sworn members together with another 15,000 in the British army. More likely is the figure that Philip Coyne, a New York Fenian whose brother Edward was a leading IRB member in Kilkenny, arrived at after a tour of the organisation in the autumn of 1864: 54,000 members. Stephens indignantly claimed that this was far too low and did not include any of the members in the British army. Regardless of his objections, this seems a reasonable total and we are most unlikely ever to have more accurate figures. Whatever the movement's exact strength, it is clear that Stephens and his comrades had succeeded in building up a strong revolutionary underground committed to physical force, under the very noses of the British.

This was a tremendous accomplishment that easily establishes the IRB as one of the most important revolutionary organisations in nineteenth-century Europe. In the right circumstances, it could certainly have mounted a serious challenge to British rule. The crucial factor was to be the 'right circumstances'.

While Irish republicans had traditionally regarded British involvement in a foreign war and alliance with a hostile foreign power as the necessary conditions for a successful rising against the British, Stephens increasingly came to see the United States as the key. The Irish in America would provide the IRB with funds, weapons and, once the Civil War which had broken out in 1861 was over, with experienced officers, men easily a match for their British opponents. Moreover, he was confident that the degree of hostility between Britain and the United States was such that once a rebellion had broken out in Ireland, the American government would look on it with increasing favour, first because of the influence of the Irish-

40

American population and second because it would inevitably weaken its British rival. While Stephens also hoped to ally the IRB with European revolutionaries and with British Radicals (he remained very much an internationalist in sympathy), it was the American connection that became decisive. From this point of view, the American Civil War had necessitated the postponement of any revolutionary attempt because of Irish-American involvement in the conflict; at the same time, however, it had seriously worsened relations between Britain and the United States as well as providing a large number of Irishmen with military experience in one of the most terrible of nineteenth-century wars. As the conflict entered its closing stages, Stephens, always under pressure from those IRB members impatient for action, decided that 1865 would be the year of the rising.

According to John Devoy, this was certainly the best time for an attempt to be made. The movement was strong and well organised; morale was high. Devoy was to be put in charge of IRB organising inside the British army towards the end of the year and had a particular knowledge of its success in recruiting Irish soldiers to the cause. These men would have had a crucial part to play in a rising. Not only would they have been able to cripple Britain's initial military response while the rising gathered momentum, and to provide a welcome stiffening to Fenian ranks, they would also have delivered large quantities of weapons and munitions into rebel hands. How strong was this Fenian presence in the British army? Much of the credibility of IRB military preparations rests on the answer to this question.

The Fenians claimed to have recruited some 8,000 Irishmen serving in the British army in Ireland and more in regiments stationed in Britain or abroad. The garrison in Dublin, according to Devoy, included some 1,600 sworn members of the Brotherhood. How reliable are these figures? Once again it is impossible to know for sure. What we do know, however, is that it took 150 courts-martial the following year for the army authorities to feel confident that they had broken the IRB's network in the army, a number that suggests a membership of at least some thousands. What is most likely in a closed institution like the British army is that there was a small tightly knit core and a larger, more casual periphery that would have rallied in the event of a rising, but that kept its head down once repression was the order of the day. Interestingly, Devoy emphasises the success the organisation had in maintaining security inside the army, arguing that despite their best efforts, the British never succeeded in identifying the Fenian centre in any of the affected regiments. Certainly, the army authorities themselves took the threat seriously enough. Sir Hugh Rose, a veteran of both the Crimean War and the Indian 'Mutiny', who commanded the garrison in Ireland, was of the opinion that if 'there had been a rising in 1865, before Military Fenianism had been properly dealt with, something disagreeable might, and would, probably have occurred'.[1]

With the end of the Civil War in America in April 1865, a determined effort was made to prepare for an insurrection. Captain Thomas Kelly, a Civil War veteran, was sent over to Ireland by O'Mahony to inspect the IRB and assess its state of readiness. His report was favourable and he decided to remain in Ireland so as to take part in the coming rebellion himself. He was joined by an increasing number of Irish-American officers, men with considerable experience of both combat and command: some 120 arrived in the three months from June of that year. Energetic fundraising in the United States was to bring in around $0.25 million by the end of 1865. Preparations were made to equip ships to carry munitions and reinforcements to the rebel forces once the rising was underway and then to harry British merchant shipping. A rising seemed inevitable, and as September arrived popular expectations grew.

The British struck first. On 14 September there were police raids in a number of parts of the country, most notably on the *Irish People* offices in Dublin. The paper was suppressed, much to the delight of Archbishop Cullen, and its editorial staff were arrested. Stephens himself narrowly escaped arrest and went into hiding. While the police staged their sweep, British warships were stationed off the coast to intercept any American vessels carrying volunteers to swell the Fenian ranks. Still Stephens did not give the word. Why was this?

Some historians have suggested that the reason Stephens did not respond to the suppression of the *Irish People* with a rising, a rising that could have been portrayed as a defensive reaction to British repression, was that the Fenian movement in Ireland was always a bluff and that he never had any intention of actually leading a rebellion. Not only does such a view fly in the face of Stephens' years of building the Fenian underground, it also fails to appreciate the nature of the difficulties and dilemmas that confront revolutionaries, difficulties that are different in kind from those that face constitutional politicians. Stephens was the architect of a powerful secret revolutionary movement and was determined that it should not show its hand until it had a serious prospect of success. To act prematurely would risk the organisation's complete destruction and in September there seemed good reasons for caution. First of all, it was clear that the IRB had been successfully penetrated by British agents and it was necessary to assess the extent of this problem. The most notable spy was a former schoolteacher, Pierce Nagle, who worked in the *Irish People* office and had acted as a courier on a number of occasions. In fact, it does seem in retrospect that

Stephens overreacted and went on the defensive for fear that the whole organisation was compromised. This was not the case. The raid on the *Irish People* hardly required the assistance of a master spy. Indeed, the IRB was organised in such a way as successfully to limit the extent of British penetration so that the authorities only had knowledge of parts of the organisation and no real idea of its true extent, much of it remaining unknown to them. But what of Stephens himself? How shaken was he by the arrest of the likes of Luby, O'Leary and O'Donovon Rossa? According to Sir Hugh Rose, Stephens began to think and act more as a fugitive than as the leader of an imminent rising. Too much should not be made of this, however.

More important were his concerns about the condition of the American wing of the movement, the Fenian Brotherhood, and whether it would be capable of coming to the assistance of the rebels once they had taken the field. America had a central place in Stephens' strategic thinking at this time, but far from every effort being made to assist the revolutionary underground in Ireland, the American movement was increasingly divided into hostile factions. This culminated in October at the Fenian Brotherhood's Philadelphia Convention where O'Mahony was defeated and the so-called Roberts faction carried the day. The decision was taken to use the movement's considerable resources to invade Canada, a fatal diversion as far as prospects for an Irish rising were concerned.

Were developments in America just an excuse to avoid taking action? Obviously, the answer comes down to one's assessment of Stephens. What is clear, however, is that without significant Irish-American assistance, any rising in Ireland was likely to be a forlorn hope. Stephens was not prepared to throw the IRB away in such an enterprise.

The Heaviest Blow

Stephens himself was captured by the police on 11 November, a coup enthusiastically welcomed by Lord Wodehouse, the Viceroy, as 'the heaviest blow we have yet struck against the seditious faction'. Two days later an attempt was made to assassinate one of the detectives involved in his arrest, but the man was only wounded. This was very much an independent act carried out without the sanction of the organisation, which rejected such methods at this time. The following year an 'assassination circle' was in fact set up and it did indeed shoot a number of informers, but it was never as effective in this respect as Michael Collins and the Irish Republican Army were to be during the War of Independence. Meanwhile, Stephens was replaced at the head of the IRB by General Francis Millen, a former officer in the Mexican army. He, together with the organisation's military council, which included both Thomas Kelly and John Devoy, determined on a rising before the end of the year regardless of the American situation. The decisive factor as far as they were concerned was the Fenian presence inside the British army. Stephens made clear his opposition to this decision from prison, and then on 24 November he escaped.

Stephens broke out of Richmond Jail with the assistance of two Fenian jailers, John Breslin and Daniel Byrne. He was spirited away into hiding by Kelly, and all the efforts of the police failed to track him down. What the escape highlighted was the extent of the IRB's penetration of the police, the prison service and government departments generally. This was the other side of the coin to British penetration of the IRB. The exact extent of the Fenian presence in government departments will never be known, but it certainly existed. As well as John Breslin in the prison service, there were two more Breslin brothers, both staunch Fenians, in the police. There were certainly many more Fenians and Fenian sympathisers in positions where they could be of assistance to the movement.

The Stephens escape was a tremendous blow to the British and a triumphant encouragement to the Fenians. Lord Wodehouse wrote pessimistically that 'the work of months is undone in a moment, and I expect more trouble than ever with much less hope of success'. Panic momentarily gripped the British and there was a widespread fear that Stephens would now put himself at the head of a rebellion that could spring up from anywhere. For the Fenians, Stephens' Robin Hood exploit gave them renewed heart, restoring morale and convincing many that success was certain. Stephens' own prestige had never been higher; his successful defiance of the might of the British Empire threatened to become legendary. Instead of using his authority to finalise preparations for the rising, however, Stephens decided that it should be postponed.

John Devoy has described the efforts of the senior Irish-American officers to persuade Stephens to launch the rising. Men of considerable military experience tried to convince him that the organisation was ready and that the circumstances were right, that now was the time. Colonel Michael Kirwin, a distinguished cavalry officer in the Union army, was particularly adamant in arguing for action. Stephens overruled them all. He would not move while American help was uncertain. According to Devoy, the organisation was ready and expectant, but Stephens' word was law. The delay was to prove fatal.[2]

Up until Stephens' escape, it seems clear that the British, for all their intelligence system, had seriously underestimated the scale of the threat they faced in Ireland. Now they suddenly found that the Fenian Head Centre had slipped through their fingers and could not be found. The Viceroy was convinced that elements within the police were disloyal and that the force could not be relied upon in the event of a rising. He urged that they should be given a pay rise, a sure sign of official panic. Experience having convinced them that they faced a serious challenge, the British proceeded to adopt more determined methods.

They were convinced that Stephens planned to launch a rising on St Patrick's Day 1866. To forestall this every effort was made to eliminate the IRB presence in the army, a task that was only accomplished by means of some 150 courts-martial. Among those sentenced to death was Colour Sergeant Charles MacCarthy, who was found to have a false key to the magazine at Clonmel, ready to hand it over to the Fenians. Sir Hugh Rose wanted him shot, but in the event all the death sentences were commuted to life imprisonment. Many other men were flogged in front of their regiments. Despite this, the British never succeeded in identifying more than a small proportion of those involved in the conspiracy.

At the same time as the army was being purged of disaffection, the British proceeded on 17 February 1866 to suspend the Habeas Corpus Act, clearing the way for mass arrests. Hundreds were taken and detained without trial: by July the official figure was 756. This was a serious blow that at least for a time effectively crippled the organisation. Stephens himself, accompanied by Kelly, slipped out of the country, crossing to England and then making his way to America. Nevertheless, while the IRB had been struck serious blows, it had certainly not been destroyed.

The split in America between the O'Mahony faction and the so-called Senate or Roberts faction was arguably the most important factor in the failure of the Fenian movement to launch a serious and effective rising. It resulted in the squandering of energy and resources that might well have proven crucial to sustaining a revolutionary attempt in Ireland. If sufficient American assistance had been forthcoming in the autumn and winter of 1865 then Stephens would have had no excuse to postpone the rising. If he had tried, then the likelihood is that he would have been overruled or replaced, as was to happen later. The attempt would have been made while the IRB was at its strongest, before the mass arrests had taken effect and the organisation in the British army had been broken. This would have been a very different affair from that of March 1867. Instead, the Fenian Brotherhood in America followed a different agenda.

American Interlude

William Roberts diverted the great bulk of the movement's resources into preparations for a full-scale Fenian invasion of Canada that it was hoped would involve over 30,000 men. In an attempt to out-manoeuvre his rival, O'Mahony decided to use his more slender resources in a smaller scale adventure: the armed seizure of the disputed island of Campo Bello, off the coast of New Brunswick. This, he hoped, would provoke an international incident and restore his position within the American movement. A ship was bought for $40,000 and hundreds of Fenians assembled at Eastport in early April, ready for the expedition. The British had been warned, however, and the island was found to be defended by six warships. Soon afterwards, US troops arrived to disarm and disperse the demoralised Fenians. This humiliation completed the destruction of what remained of O'Mahony's authority in the movement. When Stephens finally arrived in New York on 10 May, he proceeded to remove O'Mahony from his position and then attempted to rally support for an Irish rising. The Roberts faction was already engaged in its Canadian adventure. This was to consume the resources that could have been used to reinforce the IRB.

The Fenian invasion of Canada that was launched at the end of May was a far more substantial affair than O'Mahony's failed expedition. The operation was the brainchild of Major General Thomas Sweeney, a veteran of the US–Mexican War and a successful divisional commander under Sherman during the Civil War. He proposed a three-pronged invasion, with diversionary attacks being made in the direction of Toronto to draw off British troops. Once this had been accomplished, the main Fenian force would invade French Canada, where it was hoped that the people would welcome them as liberators. The plan miscarried. The forces that eventually assembled were weaker than Sweeney had planned and were without artillery. Moreover, of the two diversionary attacks, that commanded by Brigadier Charles Tevis was never made and he was subsequently dismissed for cowardice. The other was launched before the expedition was at full strength. Instead of the planned 5,000 men, Colonel John O'Neill crossed the Niagara River into Canada on the night of 31 May–1 June with a force that was only 800-strong. On 2 June they clashed with a superior force of militia at Ridgeway and successfully routed them. British losses were ten dead and 37 wounded, while the Fenians lost eight dead and 16 wounded.

Despite this victory, O'Neill now found that the US army had cut him off from the rest of his men who were assembling across the border in Buffalo. Meanwhile, the British had concentrated an overwhelming force against him. He retreated to the town of Fort Erie, drove out a small British detachment, taking some 40 prisoners in the process, and considered making a last stand. His position was altogether hopeless, however; the British could have destroyed his force with their artillery without his being able to make any reply. O'Neill crossed back over the Niagara and surrendered to the US army.

The main invasion force, commanded by Brigadier-General Samuel Spear, crossed the border into Lower Canada on 7 June. Not only was this contingent also much weaker than intended, but it confronted the bulk of the British army stationed in Canada. The diversionary attacks had signally failed. The Fenians occupied a number of townships on the border, but withdrew back into the United States as British troops approached on 9 June. The whole affair was an expensive fiasco, redeemed only by O'Neill's victory at Ridgeway.

The failure of the invasion plan led to the downfall of Roberts and Sweeney and helped Stephens achieve an ascendancy over the American wing. It was an ascendancy over a much diminished movement, however; a movement riven by factionalism, demoralised by failure and short of funds. Stephens once again attempted to postpone the Irish rising, arguing that the movement in Ireland was too weak in the aftermath of the British crackdown and that the American wing had squandered its resources in the Canadian adventure. His arguments were ignored. Kelly and his fellow Irish-American officers determined on a rising no matter what the difficulties; when Stephens would not agree, they removed him from the leadership. At a stormy meeting in New York on 15 December, Kelly was installed as Chief Executive of the Irish Republic. Preparations for an Irish rising were put in hand and on 11 January 1867 Kelly set sail for Europe. Among those accompanying him was the French revolutionary soldier-of-fortune, Gustave Cluseret, who was to take command of the Fenian army once it was in the field.

The British Connection

At this point, it is worth considering one neglected feature of the Fenian movement: its relations with British Radicalism. Stephens, as we have already seen, had internationalist sympathies. One important aspect of these sympathies was that he was convinced it would be possible to revive the Chartist alliance of 1848, and indeed serious attempts were made to achieve this. The full story of these attempts will never be completely recovered, but enough is known for us to be sure that they did actually take place.

In 1865 Stephens sent Frank Roney, a Belfast Fenian, to England as his personal emissary, charged with opening negotiations for an alliance with Charles Bradlaugh and other British Radicals. Roney subsequently recalled that:

Stephens considered it advisable to ascertain beforehand the attitude of the British republicans toward the revolt. This was most essential. Already, we had powerfully strong organisations in all the great centres of population in Great Britain. To augment our forces by reinforcements not distinctively Irish would demonstrate the unanimity prevailing among all the people of the British Isles for a republican form of government in Ireland.

Bradlaugh was approached as a leading British republican and Roney came away from their meeting convinced that in him 'Ireland had a substantial and able friend ... He assured me, so far as lay in his power, that we could rely upon the practical support of about 100,000 British republicans.' The devout Roney noted that Bradlaugh's notorious 'religious unbeliefs did not scare or intimidate me a particle'.[3] It is unlikely that Roney brought up the question of an armed insurrection at their meeting. More probable is the likelihood that they discussed the broad question of sympathy for an Irish Republic.

In his account of Fenianism Thomas Frost, the former Chartist journalist, comments on the movement's efforts to create 'a diversion on this side of St George's Channel' and argues quite correctly that this showed an acquaintance 'with the relations that existed between the Chartist conspirators and the Irish malcontents in 1848'. He quotes from correspondence found upon a Fenian suspect arrested in September 1865 to the effect that:

> every encouragement should be given to revive the Chartists. It can be shown to the working men of England, that if Ireland were independent, the Irish workmen could get plenty of work and good wages at home. Freedom, therefore, would benefit the working man.[4]

These approaches to British Radicals were, as we shall see, to be renewed early in 1867.

What prospects did Stephens' plan for an alliance with British Radicals really have? At first consideration the answer might well seem to be none. The moderation of British Radicalism and of the British working-class generally in the mid-Victorian period constitutes one of the conventional wisdoms of contemporary historiography. Some factors do suggest, however, that Stephens' project was not altogether hopeless and that it would be wrong to dismiss it out of hand. While one must not exaggerate the prospects, neither should one ignore them.

The British Radical movement was always concerned with international issues. This concern extended from support for the Union during the American Civil War to condemnation of the brutal

repression of black rebellion in Jamaica in 1865; from enthusiastic support for Polish independence to the idolisation of Garibaldi;
from the execration of the tyrant Napoleon III to fervent support
for Italian nationalism. This interest in international affairs was not
confined to a small circle of middle-class Radicals, but had mass
popular appeal. When Garibaldi visited London in April 1864 he
was greeted by a massive demonstration of support. Over 50,000
workmen marched behind their trade banners, much to the dis-
pleasure of the British government. Moreover, this support extended
even to armed revolt and, for some, to assassination. A British Legion
had fought with Garibaldi in Italy and a number of British Radicals
were deeply implicated in the affairs of various Italian secret
societies. George Jacob Holyoake and Thomas Allsop, both former
Chartists, were involved in Felice Orsini's unsuccessful attempt to
assassinate Napoleon III in January 1858. Holyoake had actually
tested the type of bomb that the conspirators intended to use,
although he was subsequently to deny that he knew it was intended
for an assassination attempt. He describes himself as being at this
time 'a connoisseur of assassination', but only in response to 'irremediable oppression.' Charles Bradlaugh was also involved with
Italian revolutionaries, and on a number of occasions acted as a
courier for Mazzini, carrying secret despatches to Italy. On one
occasion the Papal police attempted to remove him from his ship
in Civita Vecchia, the port of Rome, and he held them off with a
revolver. Of course, it is important not to exaggerate the extent of
Radical involvement with Continental revolutionaries, but at the
same time it is absolutely clear that in the 1860s there were still
influential Radicals who were prepared to condone the use of
physical force in extreme circumstances.

Another feature of this supposedly contented period of British
history is the existence of 'Ultra-Radical' elements within the
working-class. Their restlessness was a permanent characteristic,
but it only became fully visible on occasions of popular disturbance.
One such occasion was the rioting in Hyde Park that accompanied
Lord Robert Grosvenor's Sunday Trading Bill of 1855. For three
consecutive Sundays in late June and early July working-class
crowds mobbed the wealthy and clashed with the police. These
clashes came to a head on 8 July when, according to the historian
S. Maccoby, 'the Ultra-Radicals and Chartists of Finsbury,
Shoreditch and Bethnal Green organised almost a mass invasion
of the Park' and then, 'not content with the domination of the Park,
carried street-rioting and window-breaking demonstrations against
the "hypocritical" rich throughout many of the "aristocratic" streets
in its neighbourhood'. Thomas Frost, a veteran of such con-
frontations, was present that day and later recalled that many men
had been carrying clubs. There were people with bundles of stout

sticks which they were selling to those demonstrators who had arrived unarmed. Bradlaugh, at this time a novice in such affairs, was also present, and later recalled his defiance of the police as 'a first step in a course in which I have never wavered'. Only the withdrawal of the Bill and the promise of an inquiry into the conduct of the police brought the situation under control.

Maccoby situates the 'Ultra-Radical' section of the working-class in its wider context:

> It was this Ultra-Radical 'infidel' camp which supplied the most determined Hyde Park demonstrators of the 1866–67 Reform agitation, which attempted the 'Republican movement' of 1870–73 under Bradlaugh's leadership, and which manned the Radical clubs of the 80s where British Socialism was born. But possessing no avowed Parliamentary representation until Bradlaugh entered the House of Commons, it could only have attempted a successful political initiative in revolutionary circumstances, circumstances like those that were found in Paris in 1848 and 1871. British politics, of course, never furnished these.

It was to this camp that Stephens looked for an alliance.[6]

Relations between the British Radicals and the Irish living in Britain, the Fenians among them included, did not run smoothly, however. Irish Catholics, who regarded Garibaldi as a manifestation of the Antichrist, bitterly opposed the support that British Radicals gave him. When a Radical meeting was held in Hyde Park late in September 1862 to express working-class support for Garibaldi, it was attacked by a large crowd of Irish Catholics. A similar meeting the following week was also attacked. In one scuffle on this occasion, an outraged Irishman tried to stab the ubiquitous Bradlaugh. That there were Fenians actively involved in organising these attacks helped boost the movement's London membership. Clearly an alliance between these two disparate movements would not be easy.

The Reform League

Prospects seemed most promising during the agitation conducted by the Reform League for the extension of the franchise to the working-class. This reached a climax in the summer of 1866, with a series of demonstrations and meetings intended to culminate in a massive national demonstration in Hyde Park on 23 July. The demonstration was banned and the League executive resolved on a symbolic challenge. On the 23rd the League leaders duly attempted to gain access to the park; when this was denied, they went off to hold the demonstration in Trafalgar Square. Large crowds remained

outside the park, taunting the police, and eventually the railings
gave way. The crowd surged into the park and began fighting with
the police. According to Henry Broadhurst, an active and enthusiastic participant in the riot and later a Liberal MP, the police 'were
swept aside like flies before a waiter's napkin'. The crowd was, he
believed, 'in just the mood which, if provoked too widely, leads to
desperate deeds and revolution'. For weeks afterwards, Broadhurst
jubilantly recalled, there were still to be seen 'constables about King
Street Police Station with their arms in slings and their heads in
bandages'.[7] Among those injured was the Metropolitan Police
Commissioner, Sir Richard Mayne, who was felled from his horse
by a well-directed stone. Another policeman subsequently died from
his injuries. Only with the assistance of troops was the park finally
cleared. For the next three days working-class crowds continued
to invade Hyde Park, clashing with the police, but both the Reform
League leadership and the government backed away from further
confrontation.

Stephens' search for allies extended beyond the camp of the British
Radicals into that of the European revolutionary movement. In May
1866, while in New York, he joined the International Working Men's
Association (IWMA) and enlisted the support of its American
agent, Cesar Orsini, the half-brother of the Felice Orsini who had
been executed for his attempt on Napoleon III's life in 1858. More
important was his meeting with the French revolutionary, Gustave
Cluseret, to whom he offered command of the Fenian forces in
Ireland. Closeret accepted, but only with the proviso that he would
not take command until there were 10,000 armed men in the field.
This was an important development. Cluseret was a very experienced soldier whose varied career had involved service in the
French army against the working-class revolt in Paris in June 1848,
in Algeria and in the Crimea; he had fought with Garibaldi in Italy
in 1859–60 and had served as a Brigadier-General in the Union
army during the American Civil War. After the Fenian episode, he
was to take part in Bakunin's abortive rising in Lyons and his
career as a revolutionary soldier-of-fortune culminated with the
command of the army of the Paris Commune in 1871. He brought
with him into the Fenian movement two other European revolutionaries, both veterans of the American Civil War: Octave Fariola
and Victor Vifquain. Together with the Irish-American Civil War
veterans, these men constituted an experienced military leadership
that was easily a match for the British army command in Ireland.

Meanwhile, Kelly and his comrades had finally arrived in England
and established their provisional government of the Irish Republic
off the Tottenham Court Road in London. Kelly shared Stephens'
views on the need for an alliance with the British Radical movement.

He charged Cluseret with approaching the leaders of the Reform League. This little-known overture had a mixed reception.

According to Howard Evans in his biography of William Randal Cremer, one of the Reform League leaders, Cluseret approached Cremer, Robert Hartwell and George Odger and offered to put 'at their disposal 2,000 Fenians, armed and equipped with revolvers, with knives and batons ferres, 500 of them being also armed with carbines'. According to Evans, the offer was declined because in the event of the British government conceding electoral reform, 'the insurrection would consist of only the Fenians and a few hundred workmen'. However, if reform were not forthcoming then they 'would gladly accept General Cluseret's offer'. Cremer was later to deny that he gave Cluseret any encouragement.[8] Another leading figure in the Reform League, John Bedford Leno, provided a different account of Cluseret's approach:

> I received a circular from a well-known member of the Reform League calling upon me to attend a meeting at the White Horse, Rathbone Place, in order to meet M. Cluseret. On my arriving, I was shown into a private room, where I found a dozen of my confrères. The Chairman announced the purport of our being called together. It was none other than to create civil war. Cluseret, who followed, said he was in a position to command at least two thousand sworn members of the Fenian body, and on our consenting to join him, would act as leader. I was the first person to attempt a reply, in which I denounced the proposal, stating that if proceeded with, it should surely lead to our discomfiture and transportation. I, moreover, stated it was my firm belief that the government would surely be made acquainted with our secret ... and declared my intention of getting out of the place as soon as possible. Others agreed with my view of the matter, and the room was soon cleared of those present.

According to Leno, George Odger was certainly one of those 'favourable to the views of the French adventurer.'[9]

Cluseret's own account described how he quickly became aware of the ill-preparedness of the movement in Ireland, where there was no shortage of men but very few weapons. He pinned his hopes on an alliance with the Reform League: 'I saw at once that I was on the wrong tack, and that the Irish Question could only be settled by English co-operation.' He went on:

> I met with sympathy as warm with Ireland and her federal enfranchisement amongst old Chartists to whom I had brought letters of introduction, as I did amongst the members of the Reform League. I had even a nocturnal interview with members of the Executive Committee; in the course of which I was

assured that if the Irish desired to join hand in hand with them, they would certainly be welcome; and that they would make a platform which should be acceptable to both parties. I communicated these proposals to the most influential members of the Provisional Fenian Government. The most intelligent amongst them were of the opinion that it would be well to come to an understanding: others, the more narrow-minded, would listen to nothing except the 'Irish centres'. I cut these short, and, taking with me men the most highly influential as well as belonging to the highest class in the Fenian hierarchy, I repaired with them to the house of one of the most important members of the Committee of the Reform League, and there the basis of an agreement between Fenianism and the Reform League was agreed upon.[10]

While there are obvious discrepancies in these accounts, there can nevertheless be no doubt that the leaders of the Reform League did indeed temporise with Fenianism, and that at least some of them did more than temporise. It seems clear that a number of leading British Radicals were more prepared to consider the use of force to win the vote and to ally with the Fenians at this time than they would later care to admit. As far as Cluseret was concerned, it seems that he believed some sort of violent confrontation between the government and the Reform League to be inevitable. Any Radical mass movement challenging a government on such a fundamental issue on the Continent was certain to be physically crushed; troops would be used to put it down and violent disorder would be the result. It was inconceivable that the government would actually give ground and even make concessions. In these circumstances a Reform League–Fenian alliance was almost bound to come about. He was, of course, confusing the realities of British politics with those of the Continent.

Proclaiming the Republic

Initially the rising in Ireland had been planned for 11 February 1867, but Kelly felt that this was premature and issued a postponement. A breakaway faction led by the Irish-American John McCafferty refused to abide by this decision and went ahead with its own *coup de main* in England. Its members intended to size Chester Castle, capture the arms stored there, hijack a train to carry them to Holyhead, and then seize a ship to carry them across to Ireland. McCafferty had served in the Confederate army as one of Morgan's Raiders, and this plan had all the hallmarks of one of their forays. On 11 February over 1,000 Fenians from all over the north of England, many of them armed, assembled in Chester for the attack, but they had been betrayed and the town was full of troops. The operation was abandoned and the Fenians dispersed without incident, although a number of them, including McCafferty, were later arrested. While the operation miscarried, it still stands as an impressive demonstration of the strength and capabilities of the IRB in Britain. Only the informer, John Joseph Corydon, had prevented the plan going ahead. Cluseret acknowledged that the operation 'showed to what perfection the organization had been brought; nothing like it would ever be seen in France'. After this the pressure on Kelly to take action increased and, once more in Cluseret's words, he was 'obliged to yield to the general voice'.[11] The rising was now planned for 5 March.

Shortly before that date, Kelly and Cluseret visited Charles Bradlaugh to secure his opinion of their 'Proclamation of the Irish Republic' which they intended to issue in Britain. The document was clearly directed at a British working-class audience and demonstrates the continued commitment to an alliance with the Radicals. According to Adolphe Headingley in his biography of Bradlaugh, the original proclamation contained an appeal to 'the religious and Catholic feelings and sentiments of race that animate the Irish people'. Bradlaugh objected to this and it was removed. Headingley considered that the Proclamation read 'more like the argumentative harangue of the thoughtful English Democrat than the wild rhapsodies of an Irish insurgent'. It is worth reprinting in full:

I.R – Proclamation! The Irish People to the World.

We have suffered centuries of outrage, enforced poverty, and bitter misery. Our rights and liberties have been trampled on by an alien aristocracy, who, treating us as foes, usurped our lands, and drew away from our unfortunate country all material riches. The real owners of the soil were removed to make room for cattle, and driven across the ocean to seek the means of living and the political rights denied them at home; while our men of thought and action were condemned to loss of life and liberty. But we never lost the memory and hope of a national existence. We appealed in vain to the reason and sense of justice of the dominant powers. Our mildest remonstrances were met with sneers and contempt. Our appeals to arms were always unsuccessful. Today, having no honourable alternative left, we again appeal to force as our last resource. We accept the conditions of appeal, manfully deeming it better to die in the struggle for freedom than to continue an existence of utter serfdom. All men are born with equal rights, and in associating together to protect one another and share public burdens, justice demands that such associations should rest upon a basis which maintains equality instead of destroying it. We therefore declare that, unable longer to endure the curse of monarchical government, we aim at founding a republic, based on universal suffrage, which shall secure to all the intrinsic value of their labour. The soil of Ireland, at present in the possession of an oligarchy, belongs to us, the Irish people, and to us it must be restored. We declare also in favour of absolute liberty of conscience, and the complete separation of Church and State. We appeal to the Highest Tribunal for evidence of the justice of our cause. History bears testimony to the intensity of our sufferings, and we declare in the face of our bethren, that we intend no war against the people of England; our war is against the aristocratic locusts, whether English or Irish, who have eaten the verdure of our fields – against the aristocratic leeches who drain alike our blood and theirs. Republicans of the entire world, our cause is your cause. Our enemy is your enemy. Let your hearts be with us. As for you, workmen of England, it is not only your hearts we wish, but your arms. Remember the starvation and degradation brought to your firesides by the oppression of labour. Remember the past, look well to the future, and avenge yourselves by giving liberty to your children in the coming struggle for human freedom.

Herewith we proclaim the Irish Republic.

This is a quite remarkable revolutionary democratic document. Not enough has been made of the fact that when the Fenians staged their rising in March 1867, they called upon the British working class to take up arms and fight alongside them.

In his autobiography, published six years after these events, Charles Bradlaugh admitted that his sympathy with the Irish cause had 'nearly brought me into serious trouble' and that the Fenian leaders 'came to me for advice'. That was all he was prepared to say, however, because 'there are men not out of danger whom careless words might imperil, and as regards myself I shall not be guilty of the folly of printing language which a Government might use against me'. He promised that 'the rest of this portion of my autobiography I may write some day', but he never did.[12]

The Rising

Reports of the Fenians' state of readiness convinced Cluseret that a successful rising was not possible. While there were 15,000 sworn men ready to fight in Dublin there were only 1,500 weapons with which to arm them, including pikes. Despite this, Cluseret agreed to reduce to 5,000 the number of armed men that he required to be in the field before he would assume command. He still hoped that something could be made of the situation, both in Ireland and in Britain. The plan of operations that he and Fariola prepared was, given the circumstances, the most realistic possible. They envisaged the rising taking place in two stages. First there were to be 'meetings, riots, outbreaks during which the national party feels its own strength ... bands of armed patriots overrun their own neighbourhoods and get little by little confidence in themselves and the habit of meeting the enemy'. At this stage, the rebels would be organised in small bands of between 15 and 20 men and would carry on an irregular war against the British. Only after large numbers of men were already in the field and local successes had been achieved, cutting communications, capturing police barracks, destroying small detachments, would Cluseret assume command and the transition to large-scale regular military operations be made. By then it was hoped that the United States would have recognised the Irish Republic's belligerent status and that assistance in the shape of men and weapons would be on its way across the Atlantic.

This was a classic guerrilla strategy. Even given the IRB's battered state and severe shortage of arms, it would have presented the British with considerable problems. The plan did not set the rebels objectives beyond their capabilities and allowed them to evade superior British forces. They would have been able to build on small-scale local successes until they were strong enough to pose a more substantial military threat. Moreover, in the event of failure the rebels could have withdrawn underground once more, keeping the organisation intact. But the advice of Cluseret and Fariola was ignored.

The provisional government in London appointed the Irish-American officer, Godfrey Massey, to command the Fenian forces in the first stage of the rising. He had served as a non-commissioned officer in the British army during the Crimean War and had then reached the rank of Colonel in the Union army during the Civil War. Instead of a guerrilla strategy, he decided to go ahead with a full-scale rising, mobilising the IRB's whole strength for a dramatic outbreak on 5 March. The Fenian forces were to assemble in arms and immediately engage the police and troops in battle. This was a recipe for disaster, given the movement's weakened state and poor level of armament. As Fariola put it, the 'Irish Republic was not to have any infancy and growth during which it would get beaks and talons. It was to be born full-grown and fully armed.' He strongly advised against going ahead, but the Fenian leadership was determined that an attempt should be made. Even worse, Massey's orders had been betrayed to the British by a number of informers. Arrests were made and Massey himself was taken on 4 March at Limerick Junction. When he was confronted with the extent of British knowledge of the planned rising, he promptly turned informer himself. Even before the rebels began to assemble in the most appalling weather in the early hours of 5 March, the rising had already been effectively rendered leaderless.[13]

It was in these unpromising circumstances that the Fenian centres began to assemble such men as they could. They hoped to have some 15,000 at Tallaght outside Dublin by midday, but the rebel columns were easily dispersed by the police. More than 200 prisoners were taken, and over the next few days the police visited Dublin employers to discover who was off work on the 5th. Elsewhere there were outbreaks in Cork, Tipperary, Limerick, Clare, Queen's County and Louth. Some achieved at least a degree of success. At Ballyknockane in County Cork a strong Fenian force captured the police station and went on to cut the railway line, derailing the Dublin express. Elsewhere in Cork another force captured the coastguard station at Knockadown. Once it became clear, however, that the rising had miscarried, the rebels dispersed and their leaders went into hiding. The British despatched 'flying columns' through the countryside, showing the flag and hunting rebel forces through deep snow. By the first week in April, the government felt confident enough to disband the flying columns and return the troops to normal duties. Altogether perhaps a dozen men had been killed in the various clashes. The Fenian rising had ignominiously collapsed.

While the IRB organisation in Ireland was reduced to ruins, this was by no means the case across the water in Britain. Here Kelly remained at large, the organisation was intact and there still remained the hoped-for prospect of a serious confrontation between the government and the Reform League. The League's decision to hold a demonstration in Hyde Park on 6 May was advertised by Bradlaugh and others as a deliberate challenge to the government. The *Commonwealth* newspaper warned Disraeli and the government that if they did not concede working-class demands, they would get 'a war of the classes', 'a revolution'. The editorial of 27 April – Cremer, Odger and Leno shared editorial responsibility – referred quite explicitly to the possibility of a Fenian-Reform League alliance:

> Fenianism, so long as it is confined to Ireland may excite little or no alarm; but what would become of the ruling powers if the English democracy were to shake hands with the democracy of Ireland ... such a union has been more than hinted at.

The government banned the demonstration and the League resolved to defy them. On 6 May troops and police stood by helpless while 150,000 demonstrators occupied Hyde Park. Any attempt at interference would have involved certain conflict with an unknown outcome, so the government backed down. The Reform League leaders had been fully prepared for a violent confrontation; even

George Howell, very much a moderate, had made financial arrange-
ments to take care of his wife in case he was imprisoned or killed.
Cluseret was certain that if the government had chosen to suppress
the demonstration by force, then 'all the Fenians in London, who
are many, would have withstood them like one man, and a good
many resolute Englishmen would have aided them'. In his opinion,
the government 'was well advised to let them alone ... In France
it would have been a revolution'.[14] Instead, the government suffered
a massive public humiliation and the Home Secretary, Spencer
Walpole, was forced to resign. But while there remained, as we shall
see, considerable sympathy for the Fenians among British Radicals,
the prospect for a revolutionary alliance had passed. The treatment
meted out by the government to the two movements was too
dissimilar to serve as a basis for unity.

One last act of the rising remained. On 12 April a vessel, the
Jackmel, set sail from New York, carrying 8,000 rifles and some
40 Irish-American officers. They expected to arrive in Ireland as
welcome reinforcements for a rebellion already underway. The
captain raised the Irish flag on 29 April and changed the ship's name
to the more appropriate *Erin's Hope*. At last on 20 May it arrived
in Sligo Bay, and Richard O'Sullivan Burke was rowed out to
inform the captain and his passengers that the rising had been
suppressed two months before. Eventually some 30 of the passengers
were landed near Dungarvan, County Waterford, where they were
all quickly arrested. The ship itself returned safely to the United
States. While this expedition was always doomed, nevertheless it
does show what could have been accomplished if the American
movement had concentrated all of its resources on sustaining the
revolutionary movement in Ireland. If a sailing ship could accomplish
so much, evading British naval patrols with comparative ease, what
more could have been accomplished with the steamships that it had
originally been intended to despatch?

A Terrible Mistake

In retrospect it is clear that the decision to rise on 5 March was a
terrible mistake. The provisional government seems to have felt that
some attempt had to be made, regardless of either the circumstances
or of the consequences. As a result the IRB's most determined
members were sent into a hopeless battle under impossible
conditions. If a rising was to have been attempted, then late 1865
or early 1866 would, as John Devoy argued in his memoirs, have
been the best time, but by March 1867 the movement had been
seriously weakened by arrests, its organisation inside the British army
had been neutralised and the American wing had dissipated its

resources in the Canadian adventure. A guerrilla strategy was rejected in favour of a full-blown rising, with the consequence that thousands of men, poorly armed at best, unarmed at worst, with their leaders already under arrest or on the run, took to the field in terrible weather only to be dispersed by police and troops in the most demoralising circumstances. Some twelve men were killed, hundreds were arrested and many subsequently received long terms of imprisonment. There was no Bloody Assizes, however, no hanging of captured rebels – mainly because of the furore aroused in Britain by the brutal suppression of the Jamaican rebellion in 1865. What is remarkable is that the IRB survived this debacle and immediately began to regroup and reorganise. The struggle was not over.

CHAPTER 4

The Aftermath

The Manchester Martyrs

The fact of the IRB's survival as an underground revolutionary organisation was soon to be made apparent. At the end of July 1867 a secret convention attended by some 300 delegates from Ireland and Britain was held in Manchester. This in itself was testimony to the organisation's partial recovery from the March fiasco. The convention recognised Kelly as chief executive, determined that the IRB should from now on be a self-sustaining and independent organisation, and proposed to by-pass the still squabbling American factions by forming its own organisation in the United States, the Clann na Gael. After the convention, Kelly decided to make Manchester his headquarters for the time being.

On 11 September, together with another Irish-American officer, Timothy Deasy, he was arrested. The decision was taken to rescue them. On the 17th some 30 Fenians ambushed the prison van carrying the two men through the city and freed them, killing a police sergeant and wounding a number of other people in the process. Once free, the two men were safely hidden away. The rescue was welcomed as a deed of great heroism by the Fenians and their sympathisers, but came as a complete and unwelcome shock to the British government. This Fenian outrage on the streets of Manchester caused both alarm and anger. Instead of the Fenian episode being safely closed, it had now come back to plague the authorities once again. The police were soon engaged in a frantic but fruitless hunt for the two men and their rescuers. Eventually 28 men were brought to trial for their part in the affair. They were to be defended by Ernest Jones and W.P. Robert, both former Chartists. This trial and the executions that followed galvanised the British Radical movement into a campaign of solidarity.

The question of support for the Fenians become one of the main disputes between militants and moderates on the executive of the Reform League. At issue was not just this question, but also the broader issue of whether or not the League should abandon the attempt at achieving independent working-class representation in Parliament and subordinate itself to the Liberals. If the militants had won the dispute over Fenianism, then this would have seriously compromised relations with the Liberals. When on 23 October George Howell read out a letter from League president Edmund Beales disassociating the organisation from the Fenians, it was bitterly opposed. George Odger declared quite openly that if he were Irish he would be a Fenian himself, while Benjamin Lucraft stoutly defended the Fenians' right to use physical force in their struggle for independence. After a heated debate, the League agreed to call for clemency for the Fenian prisoners but at the same time disassociated itself from secret organisations generally. While it was still possible to secure expressions of sympathy with the Fenian prisoners, the days when the League leadership had actually considered an alliance with them were gone.

How much support for the Fenians was there among the British working-class at this time? The situation varied throughout the country: there was considerable support in London, but elsewhere relations between the British and Irish working class were sometimes characterised by bitter hostility. In his account of these years, the journalist Justin McCarthy wrote of a packed public meeting held in St James's Hall, Piccadilly, to protest at the death sentence passed on Colonel Thomas Burke, an Irish-American officer captured during the March rising: 'The Hall was crowded with English working men. The Irish element had hardly any direct representation there. Yet there was absolute unanimity, there was intense enthusiasm in favour of the mitigation of the sentence on Colonel Burke.'[1] On the other hand, at much the same time there was serious sectarian rioting between Irish and English workers in Birmingham that was suppressed only after 400 soldiers and 600 special constables had reinforced the local police. In a letter to the *Irishman* newspaper on 5 October, Kelly warned against 'the English mobs [being] further urged, covertly though it be, to any such criminal excesses', and argued that 'not only have I no antipathy to the English masses as such, but that I was partly instrumental in the organisation of an English Republican Brotherhood, with its headquarters within two miles of Buckingham Palace'. While well aware of the danger of sectarian conflict being deliberately stirred up, Kelly still expected the support of British Radicals. The situation in Manchester was particularly tense in the aftermath of the rescue. Here, according to Annie Besant, who attended the trial of the Fenian prisoners, 'the fiercest race-passions at once blazed out into flame' and it was 'dangerous for an Irish workman to be alone in a group of Englishmen'.[2]

Of the 28 men put on trial for their involvement in the Manchester rescue, twelve were eventually convicted, seven of them for riot and assault and five for murder. The five convicted of murder were all sentenced to death, even though no one knew who had fired the shot that killed the police sergeant. Within days of sentence being passed, one of their number, Thomas Maguire, a former Royal Marine who had no connection whatsoever with the IRB and had played no part in the rescue but was certainly Irish, was pardoned and set free because of the acknowledged unreliability of the evidence against him. Another, Edward Condon, an Irish-American officer, had his sentence commuted. The remaining three – William Allen, Michael Larkin and Michael O'Brien – were not to receive any reprieve.

Before they were hanged, all three men made statements professing their devotion to both their religion and their country. William Allen: 'May the Lord have mercy on our souls and deliver Ireland from her sufferings! God save Ireland!' Michael Larkin: 'I am dying a patriot for my God and my country.' And Michael O'Brien:

> My Redeemer died a more shameful death, as far as men could make it, that I might receive pardon from Him and enjoy His glory in heaven. God grant it may be so. I earnestly beg my countrymen in America to heal their differences, to unite in God's name for the sake of Ireland and liberty.[3]

In London, an energetic campaign was launched to try to secure the commutation of the death sentences. On Sunday 17 November 1867, a large working-class meeting was held on Clerkenwell Green, adopting a resolution that was to be delivered to the Home Secretary, Gathorne-Hardy, the following day. Accordingly, a deputation of 60–80 men assembled in Whitehall the following afternoon. Hardy refused to meet them, so they forced their way into the Home Office and held an impromptu 'indignation meeting' on the premises. They decided to hold a torchlight meeting on Clerkenwell Green on Thursday evening and condemned Hardy for 'refusing to meet a body of working men who have sacrificed a day's work to come here'. Hardy was absolutely outraged by this occupation of the Home Office. The police were sent for, but the deputation had left the building before they arrived. The Home Secretary confided to his diary: 'I wish I had had the chance to eject them ... I fretted with indignation while waiting for the police.' In an editiorial the following day, *The Times* condemned this attempt to convert the Home Office 'into a sort of Jacobin Club'. On Thursday evening the torchlight meeting filled Clerkenwell Green, with the organisers estimating an attendance of up to 25,000 people. The next day a deputation from this meeting travelled to Windsor to petition Queen Victoria for clemency, but it was turned away. On the Sunday immediately after the execution, a funeral procession assembled on Clerkenwell Green and marched through London to Hyde Park, where a meeting and memorial service were held. James Finlen, an Irishman and former Chartist, told the meeting that he prayed:

the blood so wantonly and unnecessarily shed would tend to cement and consolidate the sympathies and hearts of English, Irish and Scotch in one holy and invincible bond, dedicated to the regeneration of these islands, afflicted as they were by class despotism, dishonour and class slavery.[4]

Clearly in at least this part of London there was a well-organised and well-supported campaign in support of the Manchester Fenians.

Meanwhile the public execution of the three men had taken place in Manchester on 23 November 1867. The most incredible precautions were taken to prevent another rescue:

The day before the executions it was found necessary to stop the pedestrian traffic in New Bailey Street entirely: and the civil authorities who were especially instructed by the Home Office, took possession of the thoroughfare. About 500 policemen from Manchester, Salford and the county force were placed on duty ... In order to assist the civil power in case they were needed, it was deemed advisable to have about 500 soldiers in and about the prison. The latter were under the command of Colonel Warre CB of the 57th Foot. A strong detachment of that regiment had been on duty since the prisoners were committed there by the magistrates, and that force was considerably increased. There was also a large number of the 72nd Highlanders. A Squadron of the 8th Hussars was stationed in a street at the rear of the prison; and at the front in Stanley Street was a battery of artillery; another battery was in reserve within the prison. In the course of the night, a strong body of infantry occupied the railway viaduct overlooking the north side of the prison, the only point from which the building or the scaffold could be attacked. The reserve of that force was stationed in the Salford railway station.

Armed guards were placed on all public buildings, and the night before the executions took place 'many of the warehouses were lighted up, and guarded by men armed with revolvers'. These precautions were identical to those taken 'during the Chartist disturbances'. A walk through the streets produced 'the impression that the city was in a state of siege'.[5]

A crowd of 10,000 people gathered on the morning of 23 November to see the three men hanged. The entire space in front of the scaffold was filled by some 2,000 special constables. Allen died instantly, his neck broken, but the other two survived the drop, Larkin taking two minutes to die and O'Brien surviving another three-quarters of an hour. Gathorne-Hardy noted in his diary: 'All over at Manchester, and all quiet, which with the extensive preparations could hardly be otherwise.'[6]

The public execution of the 'Manchester Martyrs' caused a great wave of sympathy for the Fenians to sweep over Ireland. Those who had been bitterly hostile to them when they were a serious revolutionary threat now expressed their admiration for the brave young men who had died or were facing long terms of imprisonment. According to Friedrich Engels, the Manchester executions had 'accomplished the final act of separation between England and Ireland. The only thing that the Fenians still lacked were martyrs. They have been provided with these.'[7]

The Clerkenwell Bombing

The sympathy of sections of the British working-class that had been particularly evident in London was at least temporarily lost in the next act of the drama. On 27 November 1867 Richard O'Sullivan Burke was arrested by the police in London and incarcerated in Clerkenwell Prison. On 13 December an attempt was made to rescue him by blowing a hole in the prison wall. The explosion was seriously misjudged; it demolished not only a large section of the wall but also a row of houses opposite. Twelve people were killed and many more were injured. This disaster had a traumatic effect on British working-class opinion. As Karl Marx observed, the 'London masses, who have shown great sympathy for Ireland, will be made wild ... and driven into the arms of the government party. One cannot expect the London proletarians to allow themselves to be blown up in honour of the Fenian emissaries.'[8] Bradlaugh condemned the incident in his newspaper, the *National Reformer*, as an act 'calculated to destroy all sympathy, and to evoke the most bitter opposition of all classes'.[9] Certainly, it rallied public opinion behind a government that was increasingly concerned by the revolutionary threat that the Fenians constituted in Britain, let alone Ireland.

In mid-October the Home Office had been worried by information that a large party of Fenians planned to kidnap Queen Victoria at Balmoral, and despatched police and troops to strengthen her protection. By the end of November, Hardy himself warned the Cabinet that the Fenians were arming themselves in Britain itself and that in the event of an outbreak the police would be unable to cope. On 12 December the government actually decided to ban all demonstrations in London in an attempt to put a stop to the weekly marches and meetings being held in support of the Fenians. They feared the ban might be challenged, but the Clerkenwell explosion that same day ended that likelihood. After the explosion, Disraeli advocated the suspension of Habeas Corpus in Britain, as was already the case in Ireland. He was supported in this by Queen

Victoria. Thousands of special constables were enrolled: by 7 February 1868 there were 53,113 in London alone and another 70,561 throughout the rest of the country. The ground floor of Scotland Yard was fitted with bullet-proof glass as a precaution against Fenian attack. To help defeat this new Fenian threat a special secret service department was set up under Colonel W.H.A. Fielding, the army intelligence officer credited with having rooted the IRB out of the ranks of the British army. When it became clear that the Clerkenwell incident was the last act in the drama rather than the first, the Fielding organisation was disbanded in April 1868. By this time the panic was over. This was not to save Michael Barrett, however, who was hanged for the Clerkenwell explosion on 26 May, the last person to be publicly executed in Britain. Queen Victoria was outraged that only one man was executed for this incident; she urged that in future, instead of being brought to trial, Irish suspects should be 'lynch-lawed and on the spot'.[10]

Marx and the Fenians

Fenianism and the Irish situation were important factors in the development of the political thinking of Karl Marx and Friedrich Engels. The eruption of the Irish Question into the forefront of British working-class politics confronted them with the necessity of developing their ideas on the national question and on the right of nations to self-determination. They were to do this not from the point of view of abstract principles and theories, but through an active engagement with Fenianism and, more especially, with the British working class and British Radicalism.

Engels had first attempted to get to grips with the Irish Question in the 1840s. At that time, the Chartist movement strongly supported Repeal, bitterly opposed the influence of Daniel O'Connell and was trying to win Irish workers to the Chartist cause. For Engels this did not go far enough. In an article that appeared in *Der Schweizerische Republikaner* in June 1843 he dismissed Repeal as 'stale obsolete rubbish', 'old fermenting junk', and wrote of O'Connell's 'miserable, petty middle class objectives which are at the bottom of all the shouting and agitation for Repeal'. As far as Engels was concerned, the Repeal movement with its 'millions of militant and desperate Irishmen' could accomplish anything it chose, but under O'Connell's 'two-faced Whig' leadership, it would not even succeed in securing Repeal. If O'Connell were 'an upright consistent democrat, the last English soldier would have left Ireland long since and there would no longer be any idle Protestant pastor in purely Catholic areas or any Norman baron in an Irish castle'. The whole article was an enthusiastic celebration of the revolutionary potential of the Irish masses:

'Men who have nothing to lose, two-thirds of them not having a shirt to their backs, they are real proletarians and sansculottes ... Give me two hundred thousand Irishmen and I could overthrow the entire British monarchy.'[11]

Later, in *The Condition of the Working Class in England*, Engels discussed the impact of Irish immigration into Britain. On the one hand this had 'degraded the English workers, removed them from civilisation, and aggravated the hardship of their lot; but on the other hand, it has thereby deepened the chasm between workers and bourgeoisie, hastening the approaching crisis'. Moreover, Irish immigration also imported 'the passionate mercurial Irish temperament ... into the English working-class' and this 'must, in the long run, be productive only of good for both'.[12] As far as Engels was concerned, any divisions Irish immigration might create within the British working-class were overshadowed by the deepening divisions between proletariat and bourgeoisie and, leaving aside his homily on national character, by the revolutionary potential of the Irish. This view very much reflected the spirit of the times.

By 1848, Engels believed that the situation looked particularly promising. Feargus O'Connor, the Chartist leader, had been elected to the House of Commons the previous July and, with O'Connell dead, Engels considered him ideally placed to 'put himself at the head of the Irish party in a single bound'. O'Connor's opposition to the British government's Irish Coercion Bill:

> succeeded in rallying all the opposition behind him; it was he who opposed each clause, who held up the voting whenever possible; it was he who in his speeches summed up all the arguments of the opposition against the Bill; and finally, it was he who for the first time since 1835 reintroduced the motion for Repeal of the Union.

Engels looked forward to O'Connor's tour of Ireland in the summer, which would, he hoped, 'revive the agitation for Repeal and ... found an Irish Chartist party'. Later Engels noted O'Connor's success in showing the Irish people that:

> they must fight with all their might and in close association with the English working-classes and the Chartists in order to win the six points of the People's Charter ... Only after these six points are won will the achievement of the Repeal have any advantages for Ireland.

He looked forward confidently to 'the victory of the English democrats, and hence the liberation of Ireland'.[13]

While there is no mistaking Engels' enthusiasm here, what of Marx? He had virtually nothing to say about Ireland at this time. The reason is quite simple: Engels' residence in Britain had given him a degree of familiarity with and involvement in British working-class politics that Marx still lacked, and this inevitably involved him having to develop a position on the Irish Question. Engels, categorically, did not invent his ideas out of thin air, but developed them in response to the crucial position that Ireland occupied in Chartist strategy. His support for Irish independence involved him embracing one of the central planks of the Chartist programme. Marx, as of yet, had nothing to say on the subject.

The failure of the Chartist–Confederate alliance in 1848 left the republican cause in Ireland in temporary eclipse. Marx, by now an exile in Britain, thought it was undergoing a revival with the formation of the Tenant League in 1850, but with the collapse of that movement and the failure to maintain an Independent Irish Party at Westminster, he seems to have concluded that Irish nationalism was a lost cause. He began to develop an explanation for this failure. In an article that appeared in the *Neue Oder-Zeitung* in March 1855, he argued that Irish society was being radically transformed in ways that the Irish themselves were still unaware of. The pre-Famine Irish agricultural system of small tenures was being replaced by the English system of big tenures, and the landlord was being replaced by the capitalist. The way for this transformation was prepared by the Famine, with its decimation through starvation and emigration of the small tenant-farmers, cotters and landless labourers; by 'the unsuccessful insurrection of 1848 which finally destroyed Ireland's faith in herself', and by the Encumbered Estates Act of 1849 which sold off the estates of many bankrupt landlords. The key phrase here is, of course, that 1848 'finally destroyed' Ireland's faith in itself. This might well have seemed the case to an outside observer in 1855.[14]

Marx explored the transformation of Irish society more fully in Volume 1 of *Capital*. The details of his argument need not concern us here, but his conclusions are worth noting. He argued that the economic changes taking place would result in a continuing stream of emigration as the consolidation of landholdings and the shift from arable farming to pasture threw people off the land. Farms of 15 acres or less were certainly doomed, which would leave over a million people without means of support. And if, as he believed, farms of less than 100 acres were too small, then another three-quarters of a million people would have to go. 'Therefore', he wrote, 'her depopulation must go yet further, that thus she may fulfil her true destiny, that of an English sheep-walk and cattle pasture.' While Ireland might be politically and economically subordinated to Britain, the Irishman, 'banished by sheep and ox, re-appears on the other side of the ocean as a Fenian, and face to face with the old queen of the seas rises, threatening and more threatening, the young giant Republic'. It seems then that Marx thought that Irish

nationalism was in the process of being undermined by socioeconomic developments in the aftermath of the Famine and that the
threat to the British Empire came not from Ireland but from the
Irish in America.[15]

The International

The rise of the IRB in the early 1860s obviously contradicted this
conclusion, but the fact seems to have made remarkably little
impact on Marx. He dismissed the beginnings of Fenian activity
in Ireland as 'a very small affair' and later, when James Stephens
joined the International Working Men's Association (IWMA) in
New York, described him as 'the most doubtful of our acquisitions'.
Even the contacts between the IRB and the Reform League drew
no comment. In the end, it was the campaign to save the Manchester
Martyrs from the hangman, the working-class campaign of solidarity,
which led Marx to revise his judgement. On 2 November he wrote
to Engels enthusiastically praising the part that Odger and Lucraft,
both members of the IWMA, had played in defending the Fenians
on the Reform League executive. This letter includes a quite astonishing comment: 'Previously I thought Ireland's separation from
England impossible. Now I think it inevitable.' A few days later he
wrote to Engels again that 'this business stirs the feelings of the intelligent part of the working-class here'. Marx was still working out
his own position at this stage, however. On 19 November the
General Council of the IWMA held an inconclusive discussion of
Fenianism which was to be resumed the following week. Marx
prepared a speech for this later meeting in which he planned to
outline the economic effects of British rule in Ireland, then attempt
a characterisation of Fenianism. It was, he believed, a 'Socialist,
lower class movement', 'not Catholic', but influenced by the
European nationalist movements and by 'English phraseology'. The
Fenian cause was not just one of 'humanity and right', it was
'above all a specific English question'. He intended to criticise the
Reform League and to argue for 'Repeal as one of the articles of
the English Democratic Party'.

The speech was never delivered. He later wrote to Engels that
his health was poor and that in the aftermath of the executions in
Manchester, 'I would have been forced to hurl revolutionary thunder-
bolts instead of soberly analysing the state of affairs and the
movement as I intended.' Towards the end of this letter he goes
on to reveal the extent to which he was unsure of his ground: 'The
question now is what shall we advise the English workers?' This
letter, it is worth noticing, was dated 30 November 1867, over nine

years after the establishment of the IRB and by which time it had already been defeated. Marx answered himself:

> they must make the Repeal of the Union (in short the affair of 1783, only democratised and adapted to the conditions of the time) an article of their pronunciamento. This is the only legal and therefore only possible form of Irish emancipation which can be admitted in the programme of an English party.

While the British working-class advocated Repeal, the Fenians should continue their fight for independence, an agrarian revolution and protective tariffs against British industry. He ended: 'Before I present my views to the General Council ... I would like you to give me your opinion in a few lines.' Engels, by way of a contrast, was always sympathetic to Irish republicanism. He had lived for nearly 20 years with an Irishwoman, Mary Burns, and after she died he married her sister Lydia. Both women were strong republicans, and Lydia reputedly provided a safe house for some of those involved in the Manchester rescue in September 1867.

The hopes that Marx had of making Repeal once again a central part of the British Radical programme and of working-class solidarity with the Fenians were seriously damaged by the Clerkenwell explosion. This was not the end of the matter, however. By the autumn of 1869 an amnesty movement had been successfully launched to campaign for the release of those Fenians still in prison. A key role in this was played by the IWMA. On 24 October demonstrations converged on Hyde Park from all over London, bringing together over 100,000 people, overwhelmingly working-class, to demand the release of the Fenian prisoners. This, Marx believed, showed 'that at least a part of the English working-class had lost their prejudice against the Irish'. This was now his main strategic concern in British politics: to combat anti-Irish prejudice and win working-class support for Irish independence. On 29 November 1869 Marx wrote in this vein to Ludwig Kugelmann:

> I have become more and more convinced – and the only question is to drive this conviction home to the English working-class – that it can never do anything decisive here in England until it separates its policy with regard to Ireland most definitely from the policy of the ruling classes, until it not only makes common cause with the Irish, but actually takes the initiative in dissolving the Union established in 1801 and replacing it by a free federal relationship. And this must be done, not as a matter of sympathy with Ireland, but as a demand made in the interests of the English proletariat. If not, the English people will remain tied to the leading-strings of the ruling classes, because it will have to join with them in a common front against Ireland. Every one

of its movements in England herself is crippled by the strife with the Irish, who form a very important section of the working class in England.

This point was developed further in a confidential communication that Marx sent to the executive of the German Social Democratic Workers Party towards the end of March 1870. He was concerned here to defend the continued residence of the General Council of the International in London. While the initiative for the revolution would probably have to come from France, he argued, only Britain could serve as the lever for a serious economic transformation. Britain was the only country where the capitalist form embraced virtually the whole of production. It was the only country where the majority of the population were wage-earners, and where the class struggle and trade union organisation had acquired a degree of maturity and universality. Moreover, the General Council had its hand directly on this great level of proletarian revolution. The material pre-requisites for socialist revolution were all present in Britain; all that was lacking was the spirit of generalisation and revolutionary fervour on the part of the working class. Only the General Council could supply this and thereby accelerate the revolution not just in Britain but throughout the world. Britain was the capitalist metropolis.

He went on to argue that the point to strike at the English ruling class was in Ireland. If landlordism fell in Ireland then it would inevitably fall in England. Moreover, there was a serious chance of overthrowing landlordism in Ireland, because the struggle for land was the exclusive form of economic struggle there and because the Irish people were more revolutionary than the English. Landlordism in Ireland survived only because of the presence of the British army, so the moment the two countries separated a social revolution would break out. This revolution would not only cripple the English ruling class but would make possible the unity of English and Irish workers. At the moment the average English worker regarded the Irish worker in much the same way as the poor whites in the American South regarded the blacks. This antagonism, artificially nourished, was the true secret of how the bourgeoisie maintained its power. England was proof that any nation that oppressed another forged its own chains. The position of the International was clear: it was for a socialist revolution in Britain and to this end 'a great blow must be struck in Ireland'.

In a letter to the Lafargues that same month, Marx made much the same point:

> You understand at once that I am not only acted upon by feelings of humanity. There is something besides. To accelerate the social development in Europe, you must push on the cata-

strophe of official England. To do so, you must attack her in Ireland. That's her weakest point. Ireland lost, the British 'Empire' is gone, and the class war in England, till now somnolent and chronic, will assume acute forms.

For Marx, the Irish Question had become the central question of British politics. This was not because he thought solidarity with the Fenians was a moral duty or even because he regarded Irish national liberation as of central importance. What was decisive was the strategic importance of the Irish Question with regard to the class struggle in Britain. Ireland was, he believed, the key to transforming the British working class into a revolutionary class, to detaching it from the bourgeois order. Engels was to have made the main theoretical contribution on this question and began preparing a book on the Irish Question 'from our standpoint'. Much of late 1869 and early 1870 was devoted to this task. He finished the first chapter and compiled voluminous notes for the rest of the book, but the Franco-Prussian War and the Paris Commune intervened.[16]

In retrospect, it can be seen that Marx was mistaken on two counts. First of all, Irish landlordism was not the strategic fulcrum that he believed it to be. The Land War of the early 1880s was to result in the British state presiding over the first stage in the eventual liquidation of the Protestant landlord class in Ireland without any serious consequences for the political and social order in Britain. His second mistake was to attach too much significance to the role of the Irish Question with regard to the failure of the British working class to become a revolutionary class. The reformism of the British labour movement had other sources. It is true that the Irish Question was in the 1860s and early 1870s the issue that could have detached at least a section of the labour movement from its support for the Liberal Party. Gladstone, it is worth remembering, was not to embrace Home Rule for Ireland until 1886. Even so Marx had considerable problems trying to convince a number of the British members of the General Council to endorse his programme. Nevertheless this could have been the issue around which an independent working-class party was formed, but in the context of the times such a party would certainly have been a reformist rather than a revolutionary party; although this would have been a step forward, it would not have satisfied Marx's hopes and expectations.

The 1871 revolution in France failed to stir the British working class as Marx had hoped, and instead precipitated the decline of the International. Confronted with the reality of revolutionary struggle, many of the IWMA's supporters, particularly in Britain, far from becoming more militant, retreated into moderation. The collapse of Marx's efforts to build a mass revolutionary workers' movement in Britain, moreover, coincided with the International's failure to establish itself in Ireland.

The International in Ireland

The key figure involved in extending the International's activities into Ireland was Joseph Patrick McDonnell. He was a former Fenian, a key figure in running guns into Ireland, and had been imprisoned without trial for eight months in 1866 under the Habeas Corpus Suspension Act. Since then he had settled in England, earning an uneasy living as a Radical journalist and maintaining his Fenian connections. He was one of the initiators of the English Amnesty Committee, serving as its secretary, and was a prominent public speaker on its behalf. He became a member of the General Council of the IWMA, proposed by Marx and seconded by Engels, in June 1871, and in August was appointed secretary for Ireland.

McDonnell had some success establishing branches of the International among the Irish in Britain; the first opened in Soho in February 1872 and others soon followed. More important, however, was the establishment of a branch in Cork that same month. Here, the International tapped into a tradition of working-class militancy that as recently as the early summer of 1870 had sustained a bitter ten-week tailors' strike, accompanied by five days of serious rioting, culminating in a general strike. Now the International took root among the coachmakers, who were agitating for a nine-hour day and were soon to be on strike themselves. This development caused considerable alarm among the city's middle class, and on 24 March a public meeting was called to condemn the IWMA. Some 3,000 people attended, including a large contingent of Internationalists led by John de Morgan. They stormed the platform and the meeting broke up in disorder.

This success proved shortlived. It was followed by a deluge of condemnation, slander and harassment in which the clergy and the police both played leading roles. Some Fenians, most notably James F.X. O'Brien, one of the leaders of the 1867 rising in Cork, joined in the attack. By the end of May the branch had collapsed and De Morgan had been driven out of the city and eventually out of Ireland. Other branches were established in Belfast, Dublin and at Cootehill in County Cavan, but these too were intimidated out of existence. Soon after, in December 1872, McDonnell himself left Britain and emigrated to the United States, where he was to remain active as a socialist and a trade unionist for another 30 years.

CHAPTER 5

The Republican Tradition

'Plucking the Brand'

Looking back in the late 1880s on the events in which he had played such an important part, James Stephens assessed the significance of the Fenian movement in the 1860s. In a short, unpublished memoir, 'Fenianism – Past and Present', found among his papers, he argued that if Fenianism 'had not arisen in 1858 and the succeeding years ... it is at least problematical if the national feeling would be so strong in Ireland as it is at the present hour'. The movement literally 'saved the cause of Irish nationality from irremediable destruction', because without it 'a generation would have passed away without any uprising against English supremacy'. Without it, the Irish people might have come to terms with the 'accomplished facts' of British rule, but Fenianism 'plucked the brand from the burning and kept the chasm unbridged between England on the one side and Ireland on the other'. This, according to Stephens, was the movement's great accomplishment: not any reforms extracted from a worried British government, not any steps along a gradual road of improvement, but the keeping alive of the spirit of Irish nationality and of the revolutionary separatist tradition.[1]

Stephens' assessment was to become one of the central themes of the republican tradition, a justification for, and indeed a celebration of, successive struggles that ended in defeat. A central element of republican thinking was the notion that Irish nationality was at risk, that the distinct identity of the Irish people was in danger of being diluted by the long years of British rule into a form of West Britonism. All that prevented this was the willingness of determined republicans in each succeeding generation to take up arms and sustain Irish national identity through their heroic self-sacrifice. Even though the struggle might end in a fiasco such as that of the March 1867 turnout, nevertheless it was redeemed by individual acts of courage and defiance and, more particularly, by the heroic demeanour and patriotic resolution of the Manchester Martyrs. This theme was to remain crucial to Irish republicanism into the twentieth century, sustaining the resolve of the Easter 1916 rebels in the shape of the doctrine of the 'blood sacrifice', for example. It certainly deserves serious attention as one of the central components of republican ideology, with its function being, of course, to turn defeat and failure into some sort of victory. But while this ideological aspect of Fenianism is obviously important, others also deserve discussion. The first of these is the impact of the Fenian movement on British politics in the 1860s and early 1870s; the second is the changing nature of the movement as it survived into the next century.

We have already looked at the Fenian relationship with British Radicalism in some detail, but another aspect of its impact on British politics was the decision of Gladstone's Liberal government of 1868–74 to introduce reforms that it was hoped would fatally weaken the Irish revolutionary movement and bring about general acceptance of British rule. In Gladstone's own words, he intended to 'pacify Ireland'. The disestablishment of the Church of Ireland in 1869 was seen as removing a major grievance (it had been part of the Fenian programme) and was indeed a significant step in the dismantling of the Protestant ascendancy. It continued the process begun by O'Connell in the 1820s whereby successive British governments dismantled the Protestant ascendancy piecemeal in order to make British rule acceptable to Irish Catholics and thereby themselves eliminated the only real support that British rule actually had in Ireland. At the same time that he carried through this measure in the face of considerable Conservative opposition in both Britain and Ireland, Gladstone also found himself confronted by a land agitation in which elements of the Fenian movement, the so-called Ribbon Fenians, played an important part. This involvement of Fenians in rural districts in land agitation and 'agrarian crime' was to become increasingly important from 1868 onwards, culminating in the Land War of the early 1880s. The number of agrarian outrages in Ireland increased dramatically from 123 in 1867 to 1,329 in 1870, prompting two Coercion Acts and Gladstone's 1870 Land Act. That the failed movement of the 1860s could produce these reforms suggests that a more determined attempt when the movement was at its greatest strength, even if that too had failed, would have been likely to produce greater concessions.

The IRB

What of the IRB itself, however? The organisation survived repression and defeat, and under a new collective leadership, the Supreme Council, was successfully reorganised in 1869. The Supreme Council set about rallying the movement, restoring central direction, building up its strength and armaments. According to some accounts, by the end of 1870 the IRB was as strong or stronger than it had been under Stephens. Certainly it continued to worry the British, acting as a spur to Gladstone's reforms and prompting repressive legislation and the despatch of troop reinforcements in case of another attempted rising. In fact, the only major disturbance was another Fenian attempt to invade Canada in May 1870, which the British repulsed without any difficulty. However successful the IRB's organisational recovery, it now found itself in a changing political environment that was to pose considerable problems and eventually result in the movement being marginalised. The IRB found itself coming under a severe challenge from both the developing land agitation and the growing Home Rule movement. These were to pose serious threats to the organisation's revolutionary integrity as they came to exercise considerable attraction for and influence over sections of the IRB from the Supreme Council downwards. The rise of these movements was to bring about the IRB's decline in the 1870s and complete eclipse in the 1880s.

In 1873 the IRB adopted a new constitution that committed it not to attempt any future armed insurrection until such an enterprise had the support of the majority of the Irish people. This was intended to prevent any repeat of the events of March 1867. In the meantime, the organisation undertook to support every movement that might advance the cause of Irish independence as long as it did not compromise the IRB's own revolutionary objectives. This involved a reluctant recognition that revolution was not a serious proposition in the immediate future, and that rival movements were proving attractive to important elements within the organisation. The immediate result was the enthusiastic support that a strong faction within the IRB proceeded to give to Isaac Butt's Home Rule League. Whereas in the 1860s the Fenians had not faced a strong constitutional nationalist party with Catholic middle-class support, now they did. Instead of trying to crush it as Stephens had done with the much weaker effort earlier, the IRB allowed its members to rally to the League and help build it up. This placed a considerable strain on the organisation which finally came to a head in 1876, when a majority of the leadership decided that involvement in constitutional politics was proving of more benefit to the Home Rulers than it was to the IRB. In August 1876 the Supreme Council ordered that members should withdraw from the League over the next six months. The following year, in March, four members of the Supreme Council were either expelled or forced to resign from the organisation: John O'Connor Power, Joseph Gillis Biggar, Patrick Egan and John Barry, of whom the first two were remarkably enough already Home Rule MPs. These men and their supporters were by then a powerful force within the Home Rule movement and were to later play an important part in the rise of Charles Stewart Parnell.

What is clear at this stage is that even if the IRB had attempted to follow Stephens' policy of crushing constitutional nationalism, it would have failed. First of all there were those within the IRB who would not have supported the policy (Gladstone's reforms had made constitutional nationalism – of a particularly militant variety, it must be said – seem a legitimate enterprise). Second, the Home Rule League soon developed into an organisation capable of defending itself against any attempted interference by intransigent republicans. It was strong enough, for example, to protect its meetings against disruption, sending those involved away with bloody heads. The Home Rule movement was, indeed, over the next decade to succeed in establishing the political hegemony of the middle class, rural and urban, over Catholic Ireland. The Fenians were to be either dragged in its wake or marginalised.

The problems besetting the IRB were one of the considerations behind the establishment of a joint revolutionary leadership, the Revolutionary Directory, with the American organisation, the Clann na Gael, in 1877. The Clann was largely under the control of John Devoy and Dr William Carroll. Its standing in Irish republican circles was particularly high following its sponsorship of the rescue of six Fenian prisoners from Australia, the *Catalpa* mission in 1876. Moreover, Devoy in particular was at this time completely opposed to any collaboration with the Home Rulers, so it was believed that the establishment of the Revolutionary Directory would strengthen the hand of those of like mind in Ireland. Ironically, it was to be the Clann that was to be won over to the notion of the 'New Departure', of an alliance with Parnell.

Parnell and the Land War

One important feature of the IRB in the 1870s was its changing social composition. The organisation's membership shifted from being primarily urban working-class to being primarily composed of small farmers and their sons. This shift to the countryside made the Ribbon Fenianism of the early 1870s possible and Fenian involvement with the Land League inevitable. The key figure here was Michael Davitt, who was released from prison in December 1877 after serving seven years for gunrunning. He, together with John O'Connor Power, succeeded in persuading Devoy to agree to an alliance with Parnell and to impose this on the Irish movement regardless of the opposition of the Supreme Council and its intransigent president, Charles Kickham. The 'New Departure' of October 1878 involved Fenian support for Home Rule and an obstructionist policy in Parliament, and for the land agitation that was soon to develop into the Land War, the most important social movement in nineteenth-century Ireland. Parnell seems to have given no specific undertakings in return, so that from the very beginning the alliance was a one-sided affair with all the benefit accruing to the Home Rulers. What Devoy, Davitt and their supporters seem to have believed is that an aggressive constitutional and land agitation combined would inevitably create the conditions for a confrontation with British rule that might result in armed insurrection, probably before the end of 1882. The Supreme Council was sceptical, but nevertheless reluctantly allowed members to take part in the land agitation.

The Land War was launched, at a time of increasing hardship, at Irishtown, County Mayo, in April 1879 and soon developed into a national movement. From the beginning, Fenians played a prominent role in the agitation. The Irish National Land League was established in Dublin in October 1879, with Parnell himself installed as president. It was an important step in his eventual capture of the leadership of the Home Rule movement in May 1880. Meanwhile, throughout rural Ireland the Land League became an alternative government ruling by popular support that was enforced by intimidation and violence, by the boycott and on occasion assassination. It involved an uneasy alliance between both the rural middle class and the small farmers, an alliance symbolised by the involvement in the struggle of both priests and Fenians.

The massive scale of the land agitation finally extracted a reformist Land Act from Gladstone's government in August 1881, a measure that went far enough to satisfy the rural middle class, but not the small farmers. This threatened the disintegration of the Land League as the alliance on which it was founded broke up. The government preempted this development, however, when it banned the organisation and arrested Parnell and his lieutenants in October 1881. With its leadership imprisoned, the agitation became increasingly violent, threatening to fulfil the expectations of the likes of John Devoy. In the nine months before Parnell's imprisonment there had been 46 violent outrages, including nine murders, while in the six months afterwards the number increased to 79, with 14 murders. It was, at least in part, to put a stop to this that in April 1882 Parnell called off the campaign after concluding a deal with Gladstone, the so-called Kilmainham Treaty. Once he was released from prison, Parnell set about winding up the agitation. As part of this process, he established the Irish National League, a constitutional nationalist party under his own control and free from Fenian influence.

Parnell had in fact successfully made use of the Fenians to strengthen his own position until he was strong enough to dispense with their support. He had comprehensively outmanoeuvred them, although this was less a matter of his overrated political skill and more of the strength of his support among the Catholic middle class.

If British concessions in the shape of Gladstone's Land Act had not been forthcoming it would not have been so easy, and Fenianism would undoubtedly have increased in strength rather than going into decline. As it is, it is a paradox of some note that the Land War of 1879–82 proved to be the means of consolidating constitutional nationalism rather than being made use of by the Fenians to rebuild a mass revolutionary movement. This outcome reflected not just the mistakes of the IRB leadership, mistakes made by both those who supported and those who opposed the 'New Departure', but also the class character of the land agitation and the political advance of the Catholic middle class.

The political defeat that Parnell inflicted on the Fenians provides the context for the intervention of the secret republican breakaway group, the Irish National Invincibles, a terrorist organisation led by John McCafferty, who had organised the abortive raid on Chester Castle in February 1867. On 3 May 1882 members of this group assassinated the Chief Secretary for Ireland, Lord Frederick Cavendish, and his Permanent Under-Secretary, Thomas Burke, as they walked through Phoenix Park in Dublin. Those responsible were not members of the mainstream IRB, but were among those republicans who had thrown themselves into Land League activity. Indeed Kickham, who condemned the assassinations, actually described the perpetrators as 'Fenians seduced by the Land League'. It seems reasonably certain that senior Land League figures, including both the organisation's treasurer, Patrick Egan, and secretary, Thomas Brennan, were involved, but they escaped abroad. While the assassinations had been planned before the 'Kilmainham Treaty' had been concluded, they went ahead as a gesture of opposition towards it. The repression that followed only strengthened Parnell's hand.

While Parnell succeeded in ending the Land War and consolidating the hegemonic position of constitutional nationalism, the IRB went into a steady decline under the leadership of John O'Leary, always a literary republican rather than a revolutionary organiser. There was the brief excitement of the republican bombing campaign in London in 1883–5, but this was organised from America by O'Donovon Rossa and Alexander Sullivan of the Clann. It was a futile alternative to, rather than part of the building of, a revolutionary organisation.

Only with the O'Shea divorce scandal in 1890, when Parnell was removed from the leadership of the Irish National League and was fighting for his political life, did he turn once again to the IRB for support. The organisation rallied to his cause, forgetting the 'Kilmainham Treaty' and instead swallowing his cynical protestations of rekindled militancy and intransigence. The struggle between Parnellite and anti-Parnellite Home Rule factions was to end with

Parnell's defeat and death, an end brought on by the strain of the fight. The IRB remained marginalised, by now a largely urban affair, with little influence and no real strategy. This was soon to change.

The Road to Easter Week

The IRB that survived into the twentieth century had changed dramatically from the organisation founded by James Stephens in 1858. It was much more of a lower-middle-class than a working-class organisation, with at most a few thousand members. More important than this, however, was the change that had taken place in its strategy. The IRB no longer tried to turn itself into a mass revolutionary movement capable of staging an armed insurrection with its own forces. Instead it operated in secret through the manipulation of front organisations that would now, it was hoped, provide the numbers needed for a rising. These front organisations could be controlled and manipulated by IRB members in key positions whose secret affiliation would be unknown to non-IRB members. The organisation operated in this way in both the Gaelic Athletic Association and the Gaelic League. Its activities remained of little consequence, however, until the end of the first decade of the twentieth century. What altered this situation was not the organising efforts of a new leadership made up of the veteran Tom Clarke and new men such as Bulmer Hobson, Denis McCullough and Sean MacDermott, but the changing political circumstances which were to undermine constitutional nationalism and in the end discredit the Home Rulers of the United Irish League (formed when the anti-Parnellites and Parnellites had reunited under John Redmond's leadership in 1900). This created a political space in which the IRB could operate.

Two factors were crucial: the scale and determination of Ulster Protestant opposition to Home Rule, and the outbreak of war in 1914. Ironically, it was to be Ulster Protestant preparations for armed resistance to the Liberal government at Westminster, preparations supported by the British Conservative Party, which were to allow the IRB to seize the political initiative in the south. The formation of the Ulster Volunteer Force and the setting up of a provisional government ready to seize power in the north if Home Rule was carried provided just the right conditions for the IRB to launch the Irish Volunteers in November 1913. A committee, secretly dominated by IRB members, established the organisation which grew dramatically over succeeding months until by July 1914 it claimed a membership of 140,000 men. At this point John Redmond intervened to impose his nominees on the committee, intending to bring the Volunteers into the safe orbit of constitutional nationalism, but without realising that much of the organisation was still under IRB control. The outbreak of war in August 1914 provided the IRB with its second break.

The Easter Rising

Redmond's decision to support the British war effort precipitated a split in the Volunteers, with a minority breakaway led by Eoin MacNeill determined to remain in arms. This Volunteer force was, unknown to MacNeill, effectively in the hands of the IRB. At this stage the Easter Rising was by no means an inevitable development. While MacNeill was merely a figurehead and the IRB was in control of the Volunteers, the organisation itself was far from united with regard to the advisability of staging a rising. To many IRB members it seemed foolhardy to contemplate a rising while their forces were so weak and popular opinion was so unsympathetic. Nevertheless a secret military committee dominated by Clarke and MacDermott went ahead with preparations for a rising, keeping its intentions secret not just from MacNeill but from other members of the Supreme Council known to be unsympathetic, including its president, Denis McCullough, supposedly to be head of state when the Republic was declared. The military committee planned to stampede the Volunteers into a rising on the pretext that the British intended to ban the organisation, and forged documents were procured to that effect. The motives of the committee's members were mixed, but in the end overriding all other considerations was the belief, articulated most forcefully by Padraic Pearse, that a blood sacrifice had to be made to save the soul of the nation and maintain the republican tradition. All this was of course in violation of the IRB constitution.

In the event, the Easter Rising of 1916 sadly miscarried. The really quite incredible attempt to precipitate unwitting comrades into an insurrection failed when MacNeill discovered what was going on and countermanded the order mobilising the Volunteers. Elsewhere, Bulmer Hobson, secretary of the Volunteers and chairman of the Dublin IRB, was actually held at gunpoint by supporters of the military committee to stop him from interfering with the plan. The result was predictable. Only a 1,000 men out of some 15,000, together with James Connolly's even smaller Irish Citizen army, took up arms. Even so they were still able to hold the centre of Dublin against British attack for a week. Initially public opinion seemed solidly against them and those taken prisoner were jeered and abused in the streets. The execution of the leaders and the mass arrests that followed were to change this, creating a new constellation of Fenian martyrs and helping to rally a majority of the

Catholic Irish to the republican cause. Pearse's mystical prognosis, which more level-headed men had rejected, was to be proven correct, with a little help from the British.

Why was it that the Easter executions were to inspire such a powerful revolutionary challenge to British rule, while the Manchester executions of 1867 which provoked widespread anger among all sections of the Catholic Irish failed in this respect? The key to this difference is that in the 1860s the British were determined to hold Ireland no matter what the cost, while by 1916 after years of retreat and concession they had actually accepted Home Rule and were prepared to accept a redefining of the relationship between the two countries. The period from 1916 to 1921 was to see the British trying to impose Home Rule by force on an Irish revolutionary movement that was fighting for complete separation and an Irish Republic. This was a very different context from the 1860s. Another factor was the way the Catholic middle class rallied to the republican cause, giving it a decidedly conservative complexion compared with the movement that James Stephens had led. This middle-class involvement in the War of Independence accounts for both the strength of the revolutionary movement and its later acceptance of the Anglo-Irish Treaty in 1921. Added to these considerations was the way the British played into the hands of the republicans, most notably through proposals to extend conscription to Ireland in 1918. This, even more than the Easter executions, ensured the triumph of Sinn Féin.

The End of the IRB

What of the IRB? Was its role finished once republicanism became a mass movement in the aftermath of Easter Week 1916? In fact, the organisation quickly recovered from the death or imprisonment of much of its leadership and many of its members. By August a Provisional Council had been constituted, and the following year this handed over to a new Supreme Council dominated by veterans of the rising. The dominant figure in the IRB throughout this period was to be Michael Collins, secretary to the Supreme Council and the principal architect and organiser of the War of Independence. He continued to use the IRB as a secret society, working through front organisations, in particular through Sinn Féin, the revolutionary Dail and the Volunteers, reconstituted as the Irish Republican Army. The IRB continued to exercise a secret control over the whole republican movement, a control that was to come under increasing challenge and cause growing resentment among non-IRB members, but that nonetheless continued throughout the War of Independence and into the Civil War that followed. This phase of the IRB's history has been largely neglected, but it is the key, for example, to understanding the relative independence from the Dail that the IRA was able to enjoy throughout the War of Independence. Throughout these years of struggle, the IRB continued operating in the shadows, but came to play an increasingly conservative role.

This conservatism was to culminate in the IRB Supreme Council's acceptance of the Treaty in 1921, a stance that ensured its passage through the Dail. Much of the organisation's rank and file were to refuse to go along with this decision and threw in their lot with the anti-Treaty IRA, fighting against the forces of the Free State. After Michael Collins was killed on 22 August 1922, the IRB became moribund. The organisation was divided, with members fighting in both the IRA and the Free State army, and indeed there was a widespread belief that it had actually been disbanded. This was not the case. In 1923 an attempt was made by officers in the Free State army to reconstitute the organisation, but this met with the determined opposition of the Cosgrave government. Under intense pressure, the organisation finally disbanded itself in November 1924. The cause of intransigent republicanism had already passed to the anti-Treaty IRA. This continues to be the case today.

CHAPTER 6

Fenianism and the Historians

The history of Irish republicanism is charged with political significance, not so much for what it has to say about past struggles and conflicts, but because of its relevance to the war that the Provisional IRA has been waging in Northern Ireland since the early 1970s. Inevitably, any assessment of past republican struggles has implications for our understanding of the contemporary conflict; correspondingly the contemporary conflict has inevitably influenced historians' views of the republican past. This is all the more so because today's republicans claim to be the heirs to a nationalist tradition that stretches back to the 1790s, and beyond.

What we are concerned with in this chapter is the development of the historiography of Fenianism over the years since its foundation by James Stephens. This has most recently culminated in the work of R.V. Comerford, a historian who has put forward a determinedly revisionist interpretation of the movement. Before we proceed, it is worth briefly considering the 'revisionist' controversy that has enlivened Irish history in recent years.

All historians are of course to some extent revisionists, in the sense that they seek to uncover fresh evidence, to develop new insights and to question established interpretations. A good historian continually revises his or her own conclusions, let alone those of others. What we see today, however, is a revisionism that is undertaking a paradigm shift, a revisionism that is out to overthrow the traditional nationalist interpretation of Irish history. This nationalist interpretation was broadly sympathetic to the emergence of an Irish nation, endorsed its claim to self-government, lamented the decline of Gaelic culture and celebrated the various movements and individuals that had carried the struggle for freedom forward. It involved a favourable attitude towards the various manifestations of Irish republicanism which were seen as important elements in the construction of the Irish nation and the foundation of an Irish state. This traditional nationalist interpretation contained within it both left and right wings, with different historians giving preeminence to the likes of Daniel O'Connell, John Mitchel, Charles Stewart Parnell, James Connolly, Padraic Pearse or Michael Collins, according to their political preferences.

Now this traditional interpretation is being replaced, overthrown by historians who do not see their role as helping to sustain Irish national identity but instead lay claim to a more professional detachment. Let us acknowledge, first of all, that much of the work undertaken by revisionist historians has greatly advanced our knowledge and understanding of aspects of Irish history. Nevertheless, it is the contention here that this revisionist project is fundamentally flawed. It is essentially a conservative project that seems almost always to endorse the moderate against the popular, the establishment against the rebel, evolution against revolution. We will return to this. First let us look at the development of nationalist historiography.

One interesting aspect of the history of Fenianism is that although the movement was in the 1860s regarded with considerable hostility by the Catholic middle class and constitutional nationalists, once it had been defeated its struggles were very quickly subsumed into a general nationalist history. It became a heroic phase in the continuing fight for national freedom, a fight that was best conducted by constitutional methods, but that could resort to arms if the road forward was blocked. Those aspects of Fenianism that challenged the Catholic middle class were forgotten and instead a sanitised memory of the movement was pressed into service, helping to carry this same Catholic middle class to power in an independent Ireland. A key text in accomplishing this was *Speeches from the Dock* by the Sullivan brothers, T.D. and A.M. First published in 1867, this placed the Manchester Martyrs in a pantheon of Irish revolutionary heroes who now found their memory used to sustain a constitutional enterprise they would have rejected when alive. Of course, this capture of Fenian history was to be paralleled by Parnell's unequal alliance with the IRB a decade later. This historical domestication of Fenianism has been the main victim of the contemporary revisionism whereby hostility to contemporary republicanism is projected into the past.

What of the Fenians themselves? They produced their own histories that defended the integrity of the 1860s movement but increasingly came to minimise its democratic character. Two key texts were John O'Leary's *Recollections of Fenians and Fenianism*, first published in 1896, and John Devoy's *Recollections of an Irish Rebel*, first published in 1926. O'Leary can claim the responsibility for making Fenianism a literary phenomenon, for making it fashionable with the Irish literati. As far as the movement's history is concerned, his most important contribution was the creation of the myth of Fenian anti-clericalism, successfully establishing his own attitudes towards the Catholic clergy as those of the movement as a whole. Much more substantial is John Devoy's account. He was concerned to provide a history of Fenianism that established its credentials as a serious revolutionary undertaking and celebrated the dedication and selfless sacrifice of its members. By the time he came to write his account, however, he had himself moved to the right, supporting the Treaty in 1921, and he portrayed Fenianism as the forerunner of the more conservative revolutionary movement of the War of Independence. Consequently, he was not so concerned to explore its democratic character or the significance of this at the time. Nevertheless, Devoy's history remains one of the most important works in the republican canon.

Fenianism and the Left

Historians from the left have been more inclined to emphasis the movement's democratic, even socialist credentials. For James Connolly, writing in 1910 in his *Labour in Irish History*, 'Fenianism was a responsive throb in the Irish heart to those pulsations in the heart of the European working-class which elsewhere produced the International Working Men's Association.' He was to be one of the leaders of the 1916 Easter Rising, sworn into the IRB in the days before the outbreak, after a lifetime of arguing that modern trade unionism and socialism had superseded republican secret societies. Writing much later in 1951, Emile Strauss in his still classic Marxist account of modern Irish history, *Irish Nationalism and British Democracy*, argued that while 'the special interests of the oppressed classes ... were not even mentioned' in the Fenian programme, nevertheless their political radicalism 'cut them off from the respectable classes of Irish society' because of the fact that the 'negation of the existing social order [was] inherent in the idea of the Fenian as a soldier in a war against England'. The movement was recruited 'almost entirely from among the most active young men of the lower classes'. Strauss' analysis is still of considerable interest and a new edition of his book is long overdue. Both Connolly and Strauss, however, comment only briefly on Fenianism in what are more general historical overviews. More recent is Desmond Ryan's biography of James Stephens, *The Fenian Chief*, published in 1967. Written by another veteran of the Easter Rising, but one of the survivors, this is a sympathetic account that succeeds in establishing Stephens very much as a man of the left in the 1860s and Fenianism as a popular democratic movement. It is this aspect of Fenian historiography that needs to be built upon.[1]

Another important contribution is that made by Leon O Broin. A former Irish civil servant and Secretary of the Department of Posts and Telegraphs, O Broin published what is still the best narrative history of the 1867 rising, *Fenian Fever*, in 1971. This is a work firmly set within the nationalist tradition and exemplifies its many strengths. Later, in 1975, together with the professional historian, T.W. Moody, he published an important pathbreaking documentary study of the IRB Supreme Council in the years after the rising in *Irish Historical Studies*. The following year came *Revolutionary Underground*, a book-length history of the IRB from its foundation in 1858 until its dissolution in 1924. All these contributions are essential to any understanding of Fenianism and its aftermath.[2]

The New Revisionism

More recently, though, as we have already seen, the traditional nationalist interpretation, whether in its left-wing or right-wing form, has been supplanted by the new revisionism. The key figure here is R.V. Comerford, and it is to his body of work that we now turn.

Comerford's various works have, it must be said, contributed greatly to our knowledge of Fenianism, but this contribution has been undermined by an almost perverse determination to diminish Fenianism as a revolutionary movement and instead to portray it as a social activity, as a leisure pursuit. His contribution to our understanding of the movement has, in this respect, been distinctly negative. His interpretation has been elaborated in a number of articles and books published since 1979 and has most recently been enshrined in the magisterial pages of the prestigious *A New History of Ireland*.

He first advanced this notion of Fenianism as a social activity as being the key to understanding the movement in an article, 'Patriotism as Pastime: the Appeal of Fenianism in the mid-1860s', published in *Irish Historical Studies* in March 1981. Here he argued that political and economic factors were not enough to account for the success Fenianism had in recruiting members. What was required was consideration of the movement's 'social role'. Despite the intentions of the likes of James Stephens, Thomas Clarke Luby, John Devoy and Thomas Kelly, the IRB was in practice converted from a revolutionary underground committed to the armed struggle for an Irish Republic to serve 'a social purpose for which it had not been intended. It was providing young men with a forum for fraternal association and communal self-expression.' It became 'the means of social expression for smart young artisans and clerks', appealing to those young people who 'were ready for an organisation that would provide members with a sense of personal fulfilment through identifying with their peers in autonomous social activities' and providing 'a pretext for fraternisation in their free time'. Even clandestine drilling and marching, which many might consider to be military training, were in fact nothing more than 'cliques of young men discovering personal identity and achievement in group display'. Moreover, casting all caution aside, Comerford then went on to argue that Fenianism filled a social vacuum that any other less Radical movement 'could just as easily have satisfied', although he did concede that any such movement was 'likely to become a vehicle for nationalist feeling'.

This argument was later incorporated into his book, *The Fenians in Context*, which was published in 1985. Here Comerford identifies the movement's supporters as 'a section of society that was in need of social and recreational outlets', and argues that 'fraternisation in a recreational setting was at the heart of fenianism in the early and middle 1860s'. Fenians, he contends here:

> enjoyed one another's company not only in public houses but as participants or spectators in a wide variety of sports and pastimes. The only serious military activity experienced by most fenians – drill – became their mode of pastime par excellence. Learning (under the cover of a Sunday excursion or the darkness of night) how to step in line and manoeuvre in unison at the command of a militiaman or, more rarely, an Irish-American officer, was the most characteristic of all fenian activities and it was a social rather than purely military business ... Fenianism found a following not because there were tens of thousands of Irishmen eager to 'take up the gun' for an Irish republic, but because there were tens of thousands of young Irishmen in search of self-realisation through appropriate social outlets.

He goes on quite seriously to suggest that Fenianism was a development similar in kind to the development of colliery brass bands and association football in Britain.

Comerford's thesis has since been enshrined as a new orthodoxy in Volume V, Part 1, of *A New History of Ireland*. Here he states quite bluntly that Fenianism 'flourished in the 1860s because it answered some of the social needs of a stratum of the youth in the towns of Ireland'. Moreover, he asserts, quite incredibly, that these young men 'were available to join *any* other political movement offering congenial opportunities to answer their social needs' (emphasis added). Fenianism was essentially 'a voluntary social movement posing as a military organisation', and the 'conceit' that it really had anything to do with revolution 'was abandoned even more openly by those Fenians active in England and Scotland than in Ireland'. By this means has the revolutionary movement of the 1860s been apparently exorcised and the danger to the social order and to British rule that it posed has been, posthumously at least, eliminated.[3]

What have we here in reality? At the most a certain amount of evidence that many IRB members liked a drink now and again, went on outings, attended the races, enjoyed fraternising with their comrades ... and, of course, drilled. None of this comes as a complete surprise. What we do not have is anything that can be seriously taken to establish that Fenianism was merely a pastime activity that was 'posing' as a revolutionary movement or that any other movement offering a social outlet could have supplanted it. Comerford, it seems, is simply unable to accept the fact that there was a strong revolutionary movement in Ireland in the 1860s and accordingly has attempted to explain it away, simply to write it out of history as something else. This is of course hardly a new development as far as Radical movements are concerned, but on this occasion the exercise is particularly inappropriate. We have apparently encountered a new phenomenon in the history of leisure activities: a pastime that involved smuggling arms into the country, secretly training at night in their use, infiltrating the army, being arrested and detained without trial in large numbers, rescuing leaders from captivity, shooting informers, attempting to seize a military arsenal in England, staging an abortive insurrection, being sentenced to long periods of imprisonment, being hanged in public, blowing up a prison, and of course invading Canada twice. Comerford's thesis is clearly not tenable.

Another feature of Comerford's work is his denigration of James Stephens. Now the rubbishing of radical or revolutionary leaders is hardly something new as far as historians are concerned. Indeed, it can almost be considered one of the hallowed traditions of British history, but hitherto such dangerous individuals have been at least to some extent protected from such treatment in Ireland. Here they have been seen as the upholders of the national tradition, as martyrs in the cause of Irish freedom. With the overthrow of the traditional nationalist historiography this protection has been withdrawn. This need not necessarily be a bad thing. Much of the recent work on James Connolly, for example, has given us a much better understanding of the development of his politics than we had when he was considered to be above criticism. Comerford's approach is different. What we have here is condescension and denigration which comes very close to arguing that Fenian politics derived from James Stephens' personality problems. This is, once again, a quite customary way of dismissing British radicals and revolutionaries, but is a comparatively new development as far as Irish historians are concerned.

Apparently, Fenian hostility to constitutional nationalism in the 1860s was very much a personal idiosyncrasy of Stephens, who had a mind 'stocked with clichés' and was congenitally incapable of sharing power with anyone else. The phrase 'stocked with clichés' is worth pausing over because one can just not imagine Comerford using such terminology about any constitutional nationalist, government official or British politician, no matter how mediocre. They are accorded a degree of respect, deference almost, that need not be extended to *hoi polloi* like Stephens. We are also told in all seriousness that when Stephens was a boy he had talked of becoming king when he grew up, and that although his politics changed when he got older, his desire to be 'an untrammelled autocrat' had not. There are many criticisms that can be made of Stephens, including his autocratic methods, but the story that he wanted to be king when he was a boy smacks of character assassination. As we have already seen, the conflict between Fenianism and constitutional nationalism in the 1860s was between a working-class revolutionary movement and a middle-class constitutional movement. Really all Comerford is doing is blaming this, to him, unacceptable independent working-class political initiative on Stephens personally rather than accepting it for what it really was: a challenge not just to British rule, but to the Catholic middle class as well.

What of Fenianism as a revolutionary movement? How credible was its military challenge to British rule? Comerford regards it as constituting only a negligible threat, although he does concede that in the event of Britain becoming embroiled in a foreign war (with France, Russia or the United States) and of Ireland being stripped of troops, then a revolution would have had a chance. Without a foreign war, however, it was nothing but a 'charade'. This judgement derives from his view that the movement was more a pastime, a leisure activity, than a revolutionary conspiracy. His verdict is too harsh. What is remarkable in the circumstances is how close the Fenians came to mounting a serious challenge rather than the fact that they failed. A rising in 1865 or early 1866 would have been an affair of some consequence, and even in 1867 a guerrilla campaign would have caused the British considerable problems. A key factor in any calculation of the revolutionary possibilities existing in 1865 is the extent and significance of Fenian infiltration into the British army. The argument as far as Comerford is concerned is not about numbers but about quality. The Fenian soldiers merely constituted 'an unofficered ... rank and file'; without 'a corps of experienced officers' they would have been unable to 'make an impact as a fighting force'. The conclusion is presumably that to be taken seriously the Fenians would have had to recruit the officers as well! Two points can be made here: first, mutinies seldom if ever involve officers and yet they have taken place in armies often enough to suggest that common soldiers and NCOs are not completely helpless. The Indian 'Mutiny' of 1857 would seem contemporary evidence of this. Second, the IRB was actively engaged in recruiting Irish-Americans with experience as officers in the American Civil War to take command in the fighting with the British. These men, it seems reasonable to assume, would have been at least a match for their British counterparts. Inevitably, Comerford feels obliged to remark on those soldiers who took the Fenian oath for free drink. Presumably this is another aspect of Fenianism as pastime. Interestingly enough, John Devoy in his account of Fenianism goes out of his way to emphasise the sobriety of the Fenian soldiers and also makes the point that when arrested some of them used the excuse of drink as mitigation. While the British broke up the IRB's network in the army, they never, according to Devoy, discovered the true extent to which infiltration had been successful. Such success poses problems for the historian as well as for the authorities.

Clearly Comerford's interpretation of Fenianism as a leisure activity has involved him in diminishing the movement both politically and militarily. That his is a quite self-conscious revisionist enterprise is shown by his admiring reference to Alfred Cobban's contribution to 'the demythologisation of the French revolution' of 1789. Even the Land War, 'examined objectively' by Comerford, becomes 'less like salvation and more like disaster', with revolutionaries like Michael Davitt 'endeavouring to use the crisis for their own purposes'.[4] This conservative (with a small 'c') approach characterises and, it must be said, seriously flaws Comerford's work on Fenianism. The danger is that there seems every likelihood of his interpretation becoming the new orthodoxy – unless, that is, it is effectively challenged.

Notes and References

Chapter 1: 1848 in Ireland

1. John Mitchel, *Jail Journal* (Dublin: M.H. Gill, 1913), p. xxxix.
2. Ibid., p. xlvii.
3. John Mitchel, *The History of Ireland from the Treaty of Limerick to the Present Time* (Glasgow, 1869), p. 226.
4. Denis Gwynn, *Young Ireland and 1848* (Cork: Cork University Press, 1949), p. 159.
5. Mitchel, *History of Ireland*, p. 224.
6. T.D., A.M. and D.B. Sullivan, *Speeches from the Dock* (Dublin: M.H. Gill, 1945), p. 65.
7. A.M. Sullivan, *New Ireland* (Glasgow: Sampson, Law and Co., 1882), p. 64.
8. George Jacob Holyoake, *Sixty Years of an Agitator's Life* vol. II (London: Fisher Unwin, 1893), p. 250.
9. Thomas Francis Meagher, *Meagher of the Sword* (Dublin: M.H. Gill, 1916), p. 182.
10. Ibid., pp. 338–9.
11. Charles Gavan Duffy, *Four Years of Irish History* (London: Cassel, Petter and Co., 1883), pp. 630, 638, 692.
12. Michael Cavanagh, *Memoirs of General Thomas Francis Meagher* (Worcester, Mass., 1896),. pp. 266–7.
13. Gwynn, *Young Ireland and 1848*, p. 234.
14. Duffy, *Four Years of Irish History*, p. 692.
15. Sullivan, *New Ireland*, p. 64.
16. Mitchel, *Jail Journal*, p. 205.
17. Mitchel, *History*, vol. 2, pp. 214, 215.

Chapter 2: The Fenian Movement

1. Desmond Ryan, *The Fenian Chief* (Dublin: Gill, 1967), pp. 51, 84, 323.
2. Michael Cavanagh, *Memoirs of General Thomas Francis Meagher* (Worcester, Mass., 1896), p. 419.
3. Ryan, *Fenian Chief*, p. 324.
4. Ibid., p. 65; Michael Davitt, *The Fall of Feudalism in Ireland* (Shannon: Irish University Press, 1970), p. 42.

5. Brian Griffin, 'Social Aspects of Fenianism in Connacht and Leinster', *Eire–Ireland*, vol. xxi, no. 1 (Spring 1986), pp. 29–30.
6. John O'Leary, *Recollections of Fenians and Fenianism*, vol. 2 (London: Downey, 1896), p. 53.
7. E.R. Norman, *A History of Modern Ireland* (Harmondsworth: Penguin, 1973), p. 159.
8. P.S. O'Hegarty, A *History of Ireland under the Union* (London: Methuen, 1952), p. 441.
9. John Denvir, *The Irish in Britain* (London: Kegan Paul, 1892), p. 221; Richard Pigott, *Personal Recollections of an Irish National Journalist* (Dublin: Hodges, Figgis and Co., 1882), p. 234; John Devoy, *Recollections of an Irish Rebel* (Dublin: Irish University Press, 1983), p. 50.
10. Shane Leslie, *Henry Edward Manning* (London, 1921), pp. 124, 126.
11. Jeremiah O'Donovon Rossa, *My Years in English Jails* (Tralee: Anvil, 1967), pp. 18–19.
12. Devoy, *Recollections*, p. 118.
13. William Dillon, *Life of John Mitchel*, vol. 2 (London: Kegan, Paul, Trench and Co. 1888), p. 247.
14. Devoy, *Recollections*, p. 119.
15. P. F. Moran, *The Pastoral Letters and Other Writings of Cardinal Cullen*, vol. 1 (Dublin, 1882), p. 736; Peadar Mac Suibhene, *Paul Cullen and His Contemporaries*, vol. 4 (Naas, 1974), p. 183.

Chapter 3: The Rising

1. Charles Townshend, *Political Violence in Ireland* (Oxford: Clarendon, 1983), p. 90.
2. Leon O Broin, *Fenian Fever* (London: Chatto and Windus 1971), pp. 18, 28; John Devoy, *Recollections of an Irish Rebel* (Dublin: Irish University Press, 1983), pp. 88–97.
3. Frank Roney, *Frank Roney, Irish Rebel and California Labor Leader* (Berkley, Calif.: University of California Press, 1931), pp. 117, 119, 121.
4. Thomas Frost, *The Secret Societies of the European Revolution* (London: Sampson, Law and Co., 1876). p. 285.
5. George Jacob Holyoake, *Sixty Years of an Agitator's Life*, vol. II (London: Fisher Unwin, 1893), p. 58.
6. S. Maccoby, *English Radicalism* (London: Allen and Unwin, 1938), p. 143; Donald Richter, *Riotous Victorians* (Athens, Ohio: Ohio University Press, 1981), p. 51.
7. Henry Broadhurst, *Henry Broadhurst MP* (London: Hutchinson, 1901) p. 38–9.

8. Howard Evans, *Sir Randal Cremer* (London: Fisher Unwin, 1909), pp. 46–7.
9. John Bedford Leno, *The Aftermath* (London: Reeves and Turner, 1892), p. 71.
10. Gustave Cluseret, 'My Connections with Fenianism', *Littell's Living Age*, no. 114 (1872), pp. 360–1.
11. Ibid., p. 360.
12. Adolphe S. Headingley, *The Biography of Charles Bradlaugh* (London: Freethought Publishing, 1880), pp. 209, 213; Nigel Sinnott, 'Charles Bradlaugh and Ireland', *Journal of the Cork Historical and Archaeological Society*, vol. lxxvii, no. 225 (January–June 1972), p. 13.
13. Peter Nolan, 'Fariola, Massey and the Fenian Rising', *Journal of the Cork Historical and Archaeological Society*, vol. lxv (January–June 1970), pp. 5, 7.
14. Cluseret, 'My Connections with Feniansim', p. 361.

Chapter 4: The Aftermath

1. Justin McCarthy, *A History of Our Own Times*, vol. IV (London: Caxton, 1908), pp. 142–3.
2. Annie Besant, *Autobiographical Sketches* (London: Freethought Publishing, 1885), p. 42.
3. T.D., A.M. and D.B. Sullivan, *Speeches from the Dock* (Dublin: M.H. Gill, 1945), p. 274–5.
4. Alfred Gathorne-Hardy, *Gathorne-Hardy, First Earl of Cranbrook*, vol. 1 (London: Longman, 1910), pp. 231–2.
5. *Annual Register 1867*, p. 157.
6. *Gathorne-Hardy*, p. 233.
7. Karl Marx and Friedrich Engels, *Ireland and the Irish Question* (Moscow: Progress Publishers, 1971), p. 145.
8. Ibid., p. 149.
9. Adolphe S. Headingley, *The Biography of Charles Bradlaugh* (London: Freethought Publishing, 1880), p. 213.
10. Patrick Quinliven and Paul Rose, *The Fenians in England* (London: J. Calder, 1982), p. 133.
11. Marx and Engels, *Ireland*, pp. 33–6.
12. Friedrich Engels, *The Condition of the Working Class in England* (London: Panther, 1969), pp. 153–4, 299.
13. Karl Marx and Friedrich Engels, *Collected Works*, vol. 6 (London: Lawrence and Wishart, 1976), pp. 446, 449.
14. Marx and Engels, *Ireland*, p. 76.
15. Karl Marx, *Capital*, vol. 1 (Harmondsworth: Penguin, 1979), pp. 834–70.
16. Marx and Engels, *Ireland*, pp. 143, 144, 120–5, 146–8, 280–1, 160–3, 290.

Chapter 5: The Republican Tradition

1. Desmond Ryan, *The Fenian Chief* (Dublin: Gill, 1967), pp. 325–6.

Chapter 6: Fenianism and the Historians

1. James Connolly, *Labour in Irish History* (Dublin: New Books, 1967), p. 165; E. Strauss, *Irish Nationalism and British Democracy* (London: Methuen, 1951), pp. 145–7.
2. Leon O Broin, *Fenian Fever* (Dublin: Chatto and Windus, 1971); Leon O Broin and T.W. Moody, 'The IRB Supreme Council 1868–1878', *Irish Historical Studies*, vol. xix (March 1975); Leon O Broin, *Revolutionary Underground* (Dublin: Gill and Macmillan, 1976).
3. R.V. Comerford, 'Fenianism as Pastime: the Appeal of Fenianism in the mid-1860s', *Irish Historical Studies*, vol. xxii (March 1981), pp. 242–6; R.V. Comerford, *The Fenians in Context* (Dublin: Wolfhound, 1985), pp. 111, 119; W.E. Vaughan, ed., *A New History of Ireland under the Union*, vol. V, part I (Oxford: Clarendon, 1989), pp. 418, 422, 435–6.
4. Comerford, *The Fenians in Context*, pp. 93, 125, 127, 223–4.

Select Bibliography

Twenty of the most useful books not mentioned in the text:

Marcus Bourke, *John O'Leary* (Tralee: Anvil, 1967)

John W. Boyle, *The Irish Labor Movement in the Nineteenth Century* (Washington, DC: Catholic University of America Press, 1988)

H.J. Collins and C. Abramsky, *Karl Marx and the British Labour Movement* (London: Macmillan, 1965)

W.D. D'Arcy, *The Fenian Movement in America* (Washington, DC: Catholic University of America Press, 1947)

Sean Daly, *Ireland and the First International* (Cork: Tower Books, 1984)

Richard Davis, *The Young Ireland Movement* (Dublin: Gill and Macmillan, 1987)

Tom Garvin, *Nationalist Revolutionaries in Ireland* (Oxford: Clarendon, 1987)

Maurice Harmon, *Fenians and Fenianism* (Dublin: Gill and Macmillan, 1968)

Royden Harrison, *Before the Socialists* (London: Routledge and Kegan Paul, 1965)

Robert Kee, *The Green Flag* (London: Quartet, 1972)

Donal McCartney, *The Dawning of Democracy* (Dublin: Helicon, 1987)

T.W. Moody, *The Fenian Movement* (Cork: Mercier, 1968)

T.W. Moody, *Michael Davitt and the Irish Revolution* (Oxford: Clarendon, 1981)

E.R. Norman, *The Catholic Church and Ireland in the Age of Rebellion* (London: Longman, 1965)

Emmet O'Connor, *A Labour History of Ireland* (Dublin: Gill and Macmillan, 1992)

Cormac O Grada, *Ireland before and after the Famine* (Manchester University Press, 1988)

James O'Shea, *Priest, Politics and Society in Post-Famine Ireland* (Dublin: Wolfhound Press, 1983)

John Saville, *1848* (Cambridge University Press, 1987)

Hereward Senior, *The Fenians and Canada* (University of Toronto Press, 1978)

Philip Thurmond Smith, *Policing Victorian London* (Westport, Conn.: Greenwood, 1986)

Index